California
MISSIONS

Projects & Layouts

Libby Nelson

with *Kari A. Cornell*

LERNER PUBLICATIONS COMPANY

Photo Acknowledgements
Photos are used courtesy of: © Diane C. Lyell, p. 1; © John Elk III, pp. 4–5, 12, 50;
Independent Picture Service, pp. 6, 8, 9, 61; © Frank L. Lambrecht, p. 10; © Peter S. Ford,
p. 14; © Diana Petersen, pp. 16, 25, 75, 88–89; © Carol Stiver, p. 21, 34; © Chuck Place,
pp. 24, 26, 44, 59, 62, 63, 70, 84, 93, 98; © Gayln C. Hammond, p. 33; © Reno A. DiTullio,
p. 39, 67; © Don Eastman, pp. 43, 48; © Shirley Jordan, p. 80; © Ron Bohr, pp. 82, 95. Front
cover by Jim Simondet. All maps, diagrams, and artworks by Laura Westlund.

This book is available in two editions:
Library binding by Lerner Publications Company
Soft cover by First Avenue Editions, 1999
241 First Avenue North
Minneapolis, MN 55401 U.S.A.
ISBN: 0–8225–1931–3 (lib. bdg.)
ISBN: 0–8225–9831–0 (pbk.)

Website address: www.lernerbooks.com

LIBRARY OF CONGRESS CATALOGING-IN-PUBLICATIONS DATA

Nelson, Libby, 1952–
    Projects & layouts / by Libby Nelson with Kari A. Cornell.
      p. cm. — (California missions)
    Includes index.
    Summary: Gives instructions for building a model of a California
mission building. Also includes a brief history of the missions and
their building techniques.
    ISBN 0-8225-1931-3 (lib. bdg. : alk. paper)
    1. Models and modelmaking—Juvenile literature. 2. Spanish
mission buildings—California—Models—Juvenile literature.
[1. Missions—California.   2. Models and modelmaking.
3. Handicraft.] I. Cornell, Kari A. II. Title. III. Series.
TT154.N45   1998
726'.9—DC21   97–8482

Manufactured in the United States of America
3 4 5 6 7 8 – JR – 05 04 03 02 01 00

CONTENTS

INTRODUCTION / 4

Part One – Projects / 5

BASES / 6

WALLS / 12

    made of Cardboard or Foam Corboard / 13–23

    made of Modeling Dough or Sand Clay / 23–26

    made of Sugar Cubes / 26–29

BELLS / 39

BELL WALLS / 42

    made of Cardboard or Foam Corboard / 43–45

    made of Modeling Dough or Sand Clay / 46–47

    made of Sugar Cubes / 48–50

BELL TOWERS / 51

    made of Cardboard or Foam Corboard / 51–55

    made of Milk Cartons / 56–58

    made of Modeling Dough or Sand Clay / 59–60

    made of Sugar Cubes / 60–63

TOWER TOPS / 63

EXTERIOR TREATMENTS / 65

ROOFS / 69

DECORATING / 77

RECIPES / 87

Part Two – Layouts / 90

INDEX / 104

INTRODUCTION

FROM THE LATE 1500s THROUGH 1821, SPAIN CONtrolled all of present-day Mexico and Central America, parts of South America, and parts of the western United States. The region was called New Spain and the modern state of California was then known as Alta California. To strengthen its claim to Alta California, Spain, with the help of Roman Catholic priests from the Franciscan order, built 21 religious settlements known as missions between 1769 and 1823. The Spanish government and the Franciscans established the mission system to convert local Native Americans, or Indians, to Catholicism and to teach them the customs of the Spaniards. The first of the missions, San Diego de Alcalá, was built under the direction of Spanish padres in 1769, nearly 100 years before California became a part of the United States.

Some Indians came willingly to the Spanish settlements. Padres lured unwilling Indians to the settlements with gifts of glass beads or colored cloth. The padres introduced the Indians to the Catholic religion through music. After the Indians were baptized, many thought they could return to their villages, but the padres forced them to stay and work at the missions without pay. The Indians not only built the missions but also farmed the surrounding land. Many Indians died from diseases carried by the missionaries and by travelers who visited the missions. The Indians worked long hours and led very difficult lives.

To learn more about mission life, read the six books in Lerner's California Missions series. Another way to study the mission era is to build a model of a mission. This activity will help you learn about the architectural features of the buildings and the layout of the mission grounds.

PART ONE — PROJECTS

Selecting a Mission to Create

In this book, you will find pictures of some of the present-day missions. Because many of the missions fell into disrepair in the 1800s and have since been restored and rebuilt, it is difficult to know how closely these missions resemble the original missions. Look at the pictures for ideas as you build your model. You may want to add to your project some of the details you see in the missions.

Notice that each mission has its own individual style. Some of the missions have bell towers while others have bell walls. The walls of all the mission buildings share a few basic shapes, but the facades, or fronts, of the missions tend to vary. You may choose to tailor the design of your facade to match a particular mission pictured in this book. For example, the church at San Juan Capistrano has a scalloped facade. We've included instructions for creating a scalloped facade as an alternative to the more common peaked-roof facade.

A basic mission plan included a central courtyard, or quadrangle; a church; and, surrounding the courtyard, buildings that housed living quarters, workshops, and guest rooms. Five different courtyard designs are shown in this book for your reference. For the purposes of this project, however, we have provided you with one basic courtyard design. Follow the directions in the section on bases, beginning on page 6, to draw the courtyard design on your base.

San Diego de Alcalá, founded in 1769, was the first mission built in California.

5

Materials and Supplies

Mission models may be created from different materials, each of which requires specific methods of assembly. This book provides instructions for building models from corrugated and noncorrugated cardboard (cereal boxes or shoe boxes), foam corboard, modeling dough, sand clay, and sugar cubes. Skim through the book to see which building material appeals to you. All of the supplies you will need are listed at the beginning of each project. You probably already have many of the materials you will need to build your model, and those you do not have at home will be inexpensive and easy to find. Check your telephone book for art supply and craft stores in your area. When you are sure about which models to build, use the "you will need" lists to organize your purchases.

When deciding which material to use, keep in mind that a few materials require more time to assemble than others, and some projects will take a few days to dry. A couple of the projects call for you to make modeling dough or sand clay. The Recipes section on page 87 tells how to make these materials.

The best-looking mission projects result from neat work and imagination. You can substitute materials and add your own details. Your changes will make your project unique.

Indian laborers constructed the buildings at all 21 California missions.

BASES

When the California missions were built, padres chose the sites. They paced out the measurements for the church and courtyard walls, so foundation lines were not always straight. Your model will be more precise. You will construct your mission on a base using a ruler to measure distances.

You will need to decide whether you want a corrugated cardboard or a plywood base. A cardboard base works well for the cardboard or foam corboard missions. The heavier models—modeling dough, sand clay, and sugar cube—need the support of quarter-inch plywood. To obtain cardboard for a base, find a box large enough to provide a 22- x 24-inch piece. If you choose to use a plywood base, have the store or an adult cut a 22- x 24-inch piece of board.

YOU WILL NEED:

corrugated cardboard or quarter-inch-thick plywood • pencil • ruler • X-acto knife or sharp scissors • compass

Drawing Placement Lines for the Mission Walls

You must mark the base with placement lines for the mission walls, which are the walls that surround the church and courtyard. The placement lines will show you where to set the walls. Make careful measurements with a ruler and use a pencil to draw the lines.

1. Position the base in front of you so that the 24-inch sides are to your left and right. (Figure 1A on page 8)
2. At several places along the 24-inch side to your right, measure in 4 inches from the edge and make a dot.
3. At several places along the 24-inch side to your left, measure in 2 inches from the edge and make a dot.
4. Lay a ruler alongside one set of the dots. Using the ruler's edge to guide your pencil, connect the dots with a line. Do the same on the other long side.

Helpful Hint

As you draw each placement line, label its measurement. Then specific lines will be easy to find when they are mentioned later.

5. At several places along each of the base's 22-inch sides, measure in 3 inches from the edge and make a dot.

6. On each short side, use a ruler to connect the dots with a line. The rectangle you have drawn will measure 16 x 18 inches.

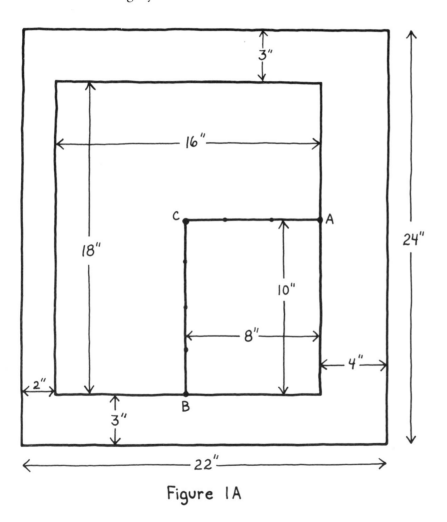

Figure 1A

A Franciscan priest uses a plan of the mission to direct the work of Indian laborers.

Father Junípero Serra, a priest of the Franciscan religious order, dreamed of setting up missions in Alta California (modern-day California). He founded the region's first mission at San Diego and went on to establish eight more missions before his death in 1784.

Drawing Placement Lines for the Church Walls

The placement for two of the church walls is already marked because you'll be using segments of one of the 18-inch mission walls and one of the 16-inch mission walls for the church. To draw the guidelines for the remaining church walls, do the following:

1. Position the base in front of you so that the 18-inch mission walls are to your left and right.
2. From the lower right-hand corner of the mission wall rectangle you have just drawn, measure 10 inches up along the 18-inch mission wall and make a dot. Label this dot A.
3. Starting again at the lower right-hand corner of the mission wall rectangle, measure 8 inches across the 16-inch side and make a dot. Label this dot B. Working your way up the 18-inch wall, measure in 8 inches at several places, making dots until you reach dot A.
4. Return to the lower right-hand corner of the mission wall rectangle. Working your way along the 16-inch side, measure up 10 inches in several places, making dots until you reach dot B.
5. Use a ruler to connect the dots. The rectangle you have drawn will measure 8 x 10 inches.

Drawing Placement Lines for the Courtyard Walls

In many mission layouts, buildings—such as storehouses, workshops, and living quarters—line the covered sides of the courtyard. On your model, the mission walls will create the outer walls of these buildings, and the courtyard walls will form the inner walls that face the courtyard. To draw the placement lines for the courtyard walls, do the following:

1. Position the base in front of you so that the church's placement lines are in the lower right-hand corner.
2. Working along the 18-inch mission wall on your left, measure in 2 inches in several places, making dots. Using your ruler's edge to guide your pencil, connect the dots with a line.
3. Working along the 16-inch mission wall farthest from you, measure in 2 inches in several places, making dots. Using your ruler's edge to guide your pencil, connect the dots with a line.
4. Working along the upper 8 inches (the portion not already designated as a church wall) of the 18-inch mission wall on your right, measure in 2 inches in several places, making dots. Using your ruler's edge to guide your pencil, connect the dots with a line. By doing that you will have created a 2-inch border along three mission walls, running from the 8-inch church wall farthest from you around the mission rectangle to the 16-inch mission wall nearest you.

Drawing Placement Lines for the Bell Tower Walls

Bells were part of daily life at all of the missions. Much as a school bell lets you know it is time to go to lunch or leave school for the day, bells at the missions called Indian laborers from the fields for meals and prayer services. Every mission had a bell tower, bell wall, or bell post where the bells were hung. Some missions had one or two bell towers, others had one bell wall, and a few just had a bell post.

If you have decided to create one or two bell towers for your mission, you will need to draw the tower-wall placement lines. Draw the

The double-tiered bell tower at Mission San Buenaventura was rebuilt after an earthquake in 1812 damaged it and other structures throughout the Los Angeles area.

lines for the first or only bell tower between the right side of the church and the edge of the base. If you would like to create a second bell tower, draw the lines for the second tower to the left of the church between the church and the courtyard wall.

In the Bell Tower section on page 51, you will find two ways to construct a bell tower—using corrugated cardboard or using a milk carton. If you have chosen to create a bell wall instead of bell towers, you will position the bell wall on part of one of the mission-wall placement lines that you have already drawn.

1. Position the base so that the church is in the lower right-hand corner.
2. Label the lower right-hand corner of the church A. Measure 2 inches (or 2¾ inches for a milk carton tower) from dot A up the 10-inch church placement line and make a dot. Label this dot B.
3. Return to dot A and measure to your right 2 inches (or 2¾ inches for a milk carton tower) and make a dot. Label this dot C.
4. Measure 2 inches up from dot C and make another dot. Label this dot D.
5. Using the ruler's edge to guide your pencil, draw a line from dot A to dot C, then from dot C to dot D, and finally from dot D to dot B. Your connected dots should measure 2 inches square (or 2¾ inches square for a milk carton tower). (Figure 1B)

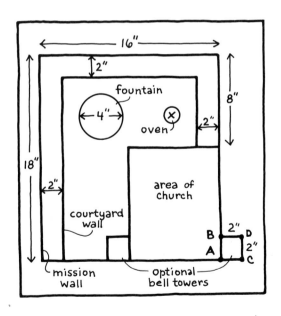

Figure 1B

Note: If you decide to make your tower out of a milk carton, measure and draw 2¾-inch squares instead of 2-inch squares.

Drawing Placement Lines
for the Finishing Touches

Finishing touches include fountains, courtyard ovens, and walkways. In mission courtyards, a tiled square often housed the shallow pool in which a fountain was centered. Because the fountain requires a specific and considerable amount of space, draw its placement lines first. Then decide where to place other smaller touches.

1. Choose a place for your fountain that is at least 4 inches square. Make a dot in the center (you can guess) of this area. Set a compass for two inches and place the point on your dot. Draw a 4-inch circle.
2. Make a dark X on the dot in the center of the circle so you can easily place your fountain when you are ready.
3. Choose a place for your courtyard oven and draw an X to mark it. The oven has a 1½-inch diameter base, so it will require that much space in your courtyard.
4. Draw 1-inch-wide walkways connecting your finishing touches to the church and courtyard buildings.

To create a lush fountain like this one at San Juan Capistrano, glue moss around the fountain base.

WALLS

Most of the California missions were built of adobe bricks. Unpaid Indian laborers, called neophytes, made the bricks from the most readily available building materials—wet adobe clay (a clay found in dry regions), manure, and straw—which they mixed and then poured into molds that were set in the sun. As the bricks began to harden, the laborers removed the molds and allowed the bricks to further dry into firm, strong blocks.

To support the brick's own weight and that of the heavy roof tiles, the adobe-brick walls needed to be 4 to 7 feet wide. Even so, bricks could not be stacked more than 40 feet high because their mass might topple the walls.

The building materials you will be using are light, so you will not have to worry about the thickness of your mission's walls. Instructions for creating, assembling, and attaching the walls to the base follow. For instructions on how to build one or two bell towers or a bell wall, refer to Bell Walls and Bell Towers, starting on page 42. Find the directions for your medium—cardboard, foam corboard, modeling dough, sand clay, or sugar cube—and start building!

CARDBOARD OR FOAM CORBOARD MISSION

A cardboard mission may be the easiest, least expensive model to create because you most likely have around the house the main material you will need—corrugated or noncorrugated cardboard. Although noncorrugated cardboard (cereal and shoe boxes) is easier to cut, the boxes are small, flimsy, and will need to be painted. Corrugated cardboard boxes are larger, sturdier, and may be left their natural tan color.

Another option is to create a lightweight but sturdy model out of foam corboard. Buy foam corboard at a craft or office supply store.

YOU WILL NEED:
corrugated cardboard base • corrugated or noncorrugated cardboard, or foam corboard • ruler • pencil • scissors or X-acto knife • crayons or colored markers • duct or packing tape

Helpful Hint

If one side of your cardboard has printing on it, use that side as the back. If neither side of your cardboard is printed upon, designate one side as the back.

13

Creating the Mission Walls

The mission walls form the outer walls of the courtyard buildings. All mission walls will be 2¾ inches high. Measure and draw one wall in each of the following dimensions. Ask an adult to help you cut out the walls with an X-acto knife.

- ▶ 18 x 2¾ inches
- ▶ 16 x 2¾ inches
- ▶ 8 x 2¾ inches

Creating the Courtyard Walls

The courtyard walls form the inner walls of the courtyard buildings. Because of heavy rains, mission roofs had to be angled to allow the rain to run off. While most courtyard building roofs were peaked, the model you are creating will have roofs that slant in from the outside.

To create your angled roof, you will need to make the courtyard walls shorter than the mission walls. The courtyard walls will be 2¼ inches high. Measure and draw one wall in each of the following dimensions. Ask an adult to help you cut them out with an X-acto knife.

- ▶ 16 x 2¼ inches
- ▶ 12 x 2¼ inches
- ▶ 6 x 2¼ inches

Creating the Courtyard Wall Arches

Arched doorways were common to the courtyard walls, providing a view of the fountain and the trees in the courtyard garden. Each arch will be 2 inches wide and 1½ inches tall. There will be a half-inch space between each arch. Your arches will not end at the same spot on each wall.

The courtyard walls at Mission San Miguel include arches of various heights and widths, a feature unique to this mission.

1. To draw outlines for arches on the courtyard walls, place the 16-inch courtyard wall piece horizontally in front of you. (If you are using cardboard and one side is printed upon, place the printed side up.)

2. Starting from the lower left-hand corner, measure in ½ inch along the 16-inch side nearest you and make a dot. Label this dot A.

3. From dot A, measure 2 inches to the right and make a second dot. Label this dot B.

4. Find the center point between dots A and B (1 inch) and make a small mark. From there, measure up 1½ inches and make a third dot. Label this dot C.

5. Starting from dot A, draw an arch connecting it to dot C and then to dot B. (Figure 2)

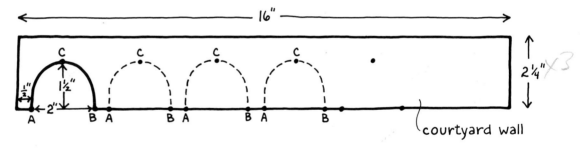

Figure 2

6. Starting from dot B, measure ½ inch to the right along the bottom of the wall and make a dot. Label this dot A.

7. Repeat steps 3 through 5 to draw the next arch.

8. Using steps 2 through 7, draw four more arches on the 16-inch piece, four arches on the 12-inch piece, and two arches on the 6-inch piece.

9. You may color in the arches, cut them out with scissors, or ask an adult to cut them out with an X-acto knife. Erase any pencil marks you made around the arches.

Creating the Church Walls

The instructions you will follow to create the church walls will depend upon what kind of roof you decide to build. All of the mission churches have a basic peaked roof, which has two halves that meet at a center point or peak. You are probably familiar with peaked roofs because they are commonly found on houses. On most missions, the roof rests on two walls that narrow to the peak.

All but the following missions have basic peaked roofs—San Diego de Alcalá in San Diego, San Carlos Borromeo de Carmelo in Carmel, and San Luis Rey de Francia in Oceanside. These three missions use the basic peaked roof with an elaborate scalloped facade, or front, that extends above the roof line. A scalloped facade consists of a series of small archlike curves that make up one large arch (see Figure 4 on page 18). If you've decided to make a scalloped facade, turn to the directions for Creating the Church Walls for a Scalloped Facade on page 17. Otherwise, create church walls for your mission by following the directions in the next section.

Creating the Church Walls for a Basic Peaked Roof

Using a ruler and pencil, measure and draw the church walls on cardboard or foam corboard. You will need to draw two rectangular walls and two peaked walls, which look like rectangles topped with triangles.

    1. On the back side of the cardboard or foam corboard, draw lines for two 10- x 4-inch rectangular walls and two 8- x 5^1/$_2$-inch rectangular walls.

Mission San Antonio de Padua has a scalloped bell wall topped with an iron cross that was brought from Spain. Indian laborers built a barrel vault that led from the bell wall directly to the church.

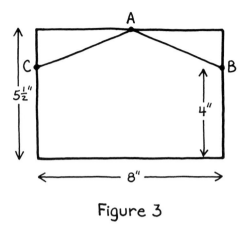

Figure 3

2. Cut out the four walls with scissors, or ask an adult to cut them out with an X-acto knife. Set the two 10- x 4-inch walls aside.
3. To create a peaked wall, place one of the 8- x 5½-inch walls in front of you with the 5½-inch sides to your left and right.
4. Along the 8-inch side farthest from you, find the center point (4 inches) and make a dot. Label this dot A.
5. Starting from the lower right-hand corner, measure up 4 inches along the 5½-inch side and make a dot. Label this dot B.
6. Starting from the lower left-hand corner, measure up 4 inches along the 5½-inch side and make a dot. Label this dot C. (Figure 3)
7. Use a ruler and pencil to draw a line from dot A to dot B.
8. Use a ruler and pencil to draw a line from dot A to dot C.
9. Use scissors or ask an adult to use an X-acto knife to cut along the two diagonal lines you have just drawn.
10. Repeat steps 3 through 9 to create the other peaked wall.
11. Choose one peaked wall to be the front of the church. Draw the outline for the doorway on this piece. You can also draw outlines for windows. For ideas about where to position these openings, refer to pictures of missions.
12. Draw the windows, if you wish, on the other three church walls.
13. You may color in the doors or windows, cut them out with scissors, or ask an adult to cut out the openings with an X-acto knife.

Creating the Church Walls for a Scalloped Facade

Using a ruler and pencil, measure and draw the church walls on the cardboard or foam corboard. You will need to draw two rectangular walls, one peaked wall that is a rectangle topped with a triangle, and one wall that is a rectangle with a scalloped top.

1. On the back side of the cardboard or foam corboard, draw two 10- x 4-inch rectangular walls, one 8- x 5½-inch rectangular wall, and one 8- x 7-inch rectangular wall.

2. Cut out the four walls with scissors, or ask an adult to cut them out with an X-acto knife. Set the two 10- x 4-inch walls aside.

3. To create the one peaked wall follow steps 3 through 9 in Creating the Church Walls for a Basic Peaked Roof on page 16.

4. To create the one scalloped wall, place the 8 x 7-inch wall piece in front of you with the 7-inch sides to your left and right.

5. Along the 8-inch side farthest from you, find the center point (4 inches) and make a dot. Label this dot A.

6. Starting from the lower right-hand corner, measure up 4 inches along the 7-inch side and make a dot. Label this dot B.

7. Starting from the lower left-hand corner, measure up 4 inches along the 7-inch side and make a dot. Label this dot C.

8. Draw a scalloped line from dot A to dot B. (Figure 4)

9. Draw a scalloped line from dot A to dot C.

10. Use scissors or ask an adult to use an X-acto knife to cut along the scalloped edges.

11. The scalloped wall will be the front of the church. Draw the outline for the doorway on this piece. You can also draw outlines for windows. For ideas about where to position these openings, refer to pictures of the missions.

12. Draw the windows, if you wish, on the other three church walls.

13. You may color in the doors or windows, cut them out with scissors, or ask an adult to cut out the openings with an X-acto knife.

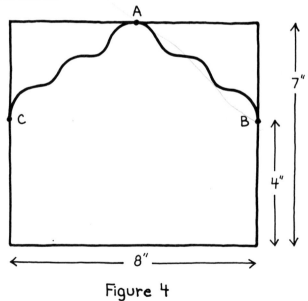

Figure 4

Creating the End Wall

1. Measure and draw a 2³/₄- x 2-inch rectangular wall. Place the wall in front of you with the 2³/₄-inch sides to your left and right. If one side is printed, place the printed side down.
2. Starting at the lower right-hand corner, measure up 2³/₄ inches along the 2³/₄-inch side and make a dot. Label this dot A.
3. Use a ruler and pencil to draw a diagonal line from the upper left-hand corner of the rectangle to dot A.
4. Use scissors, or ask an adult to use an X-acto knife, to cut out the wall.

Assembling the Walls

The first step in assembling the model is putting together each set of walls: mission, courtyard, and church.

Putting Together the Mission Walls

1. Lay the three mission wall pieces horizontally in front of you from left to right: 18-inch piece, 16-inch piece, 8-inch piece.
2. Apply one piece of tape horizontally to connect the three pieces.
3. Apply one piece of tape vertically to cover each seam. (Figure 5)

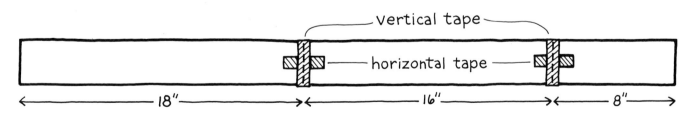

Figure 5

Putting Together the Courtyard Walls

1. Lay the three courtyard wall pieces horizontally in front of you from left to right: 16-inch piece, 12-inch piece, 6-inch piece. (Any arches you may have drawn on the courtyard wall pieces should be on the sides farthest from you.) (Figure 6)

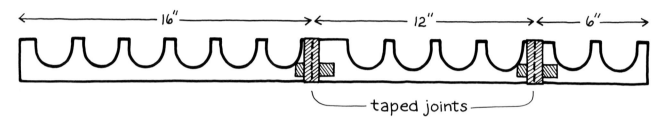

Figure 6

2. Apply pieces of tape horizontally to connect the three pieces, taking care not to cover any cutout arches with tape.
3. Apply one piece of tape vertically to cover each seam.

Putting Together the Church Walls

1. Lay the four church wall pieces horizontally in front of you from left to right: 8-inch piece, 10-inch piece, 8-inch piece, 10-inch piece.
2. Apply three pieces of tape horizontally to connect the four pieces.
3. Apply one piece of tape vertically to cover each seam.
4. Apply two pieces of tape horizontally to the right-hand side of the 10-inch church wall on the right, extending 1 inch beyond the cardboard.

Attaching the Walls to the Base

Position the base in front of you so the church-wall placement lines are in the lower right-hand corner.

Mission Walls

1. You will attach the mission walls first. Position the set of walls in front of you so the 18-inch segment is on your left, taped side up. On the edge nearest you, apply at least three 2-inch pieces of duct or packing tape vertically, extending 1 inch beyond the cardboard or foam corboard.
2. Fold at taped seams so each of the two corners is a right angle, forming three sides of a rectangle. Make sure the tape is on the inside of the right angles.
3. Position the mission walls on top of the outermost placement lines on the base.
4. Firmly press the tape to the base.

Courtyard Walls

1. To attach the courtyard walls, position them in front of you so the 16-inch segment is on your left, taped side up, and the arch openings are farthest from you. On the edge farthest from you, apply at least three 2-inch pieces of duct or packing tape vertically, extending 1 inch beyond the cardboard or foam corboard.
2. Fold at taped seams so each of the two corners is a right angle, forming three sides of a rectangle. Make sure the tape is on the outside of the right angles.
3. Position the courtyard walls on the courtyard-wall placement lines on the base. (The taped side should face the mission wall.) Firmly press the tape to the base.

Off the long corridors of the missions were storerooms and living quarters.

Church Walls

1. To attach the church walls, position the set of walls in front of you so the taped side is up and the peaked/scalloped roof pieces point away from you. In the center of each wall piece on the edge nearest you, apply one 3-inch piece of duct or packing tape vertically, extending 1 inch beyond the cardboard or foam corboard.

2. Fold at taped seams so the four pieces are at right angles to one another and taped seams are inside, forming a rectangle. Make sure all extended pieces of tape are tucked inside as well.

3. To complete and secure the church shape, apply the two horizontal pieces of tape inside over the fourth seam. Then apply a vertical piece of tape over the two horizontal ones so this seam looks like the others.

4. Position the church walls on top of the church-wall placement lines. Make sure that the peaked or scalloped wall you have chosen as the front is closest to you and that the vertical extended pieces of tape are inside the rectangle.

5. Firmly press the tape to the base. Where the courtyard wall and mission wall meet the church, secure by applying tape horizontally to the taped side (inside) of the mission and courtyard walls and adhering it to the outside of the church wall.

End Wall

1. To attach the end wall, position the piece in front of you with the $2\frac{1}{4}$-inch side to your left, the $2\frac{3}{4}$-inch side to your right, and the diagonal pointing away from you, printed side up.

2. Apply two $1\frac{1}{2}$-inch pieces of tape horizontally to each side (as far apart as possible), with each piece extending 1 inch beyond the edge.

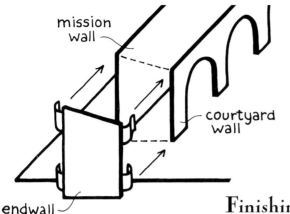

mission wall

courtyard wall

endwall

Figure 7

3. Holding the tape extensions toward the center of the end wall, place it in the opening, making sure the end wall's taller side meets the mission wall. Reach inside to secure the tape to the mission and courtyard walls. (Figure 7)

Finishing the Walls

You may leave the cardboard walls of your mission their natural color, color your walls with crayons or markers, paint them with acrylic paint, or texture them with papier-mâché. You may decorate your foam corboard mission with crayons, colored markers, or acrylic paint. Do not apply papier-mâché to a foam corboard model because the water-based paste may warp the walls. For specific instructions on mixing acrylic paints and making papier-mâché paste and strips, refer to pages 67 and 68 in Exterior Treatments.

After finishing the walls, the next step is to create a bell wall or bell towers. To learn how to make a bell wall or bell towers, turn to Bell Walls and Bell Towers, starting on page 42.

MODELING DOUGH OR SAND CLAY MISSION

Made from supplies you probably have in your kitchen, modeling dough can be ready in 15 minutes and is easy to work with. Sand clay can be made on the stove top in 5 minutes, and the cracked texture of the finished walls resembles the coarseness of the sandstone missions.

Follow the recipe for modeling dough on page 87 or for sand clay on page 89. To create the walls, you will make paper pattern pieces, place them on the rolled-out dough or clay, and cut around the patterns with a dinner knife. Make and use one entire batch of dough or clay before mixing the next batch. The mission walls you create using dough or clay will be dry and hard in 24 to 48 hours. The heavier modeling dough or sand clay missions need the support of a quarter-inch plywood base.

A white-washed wall at San Diego de Alcalá contrasts sharply with the carved oak door of the church.

YOU WILL NEED:
plywood base (quarter-inch thick) • several sheets of newspaper or 2 paper grocery bags • ruler • pencil • scissors • 3 batches of modeling dough or 4 batches of sand clay (Make the dough or clay after you have created the paper pattern pieces.) • waxed paper • rolling pin • dinner knife • spatula • cookie sheet(s) • small cross • duct tape • earthen red acrylic paint (optional) • small paintbrush (optional)

Creating the Paper Pattern Pieces

Substituting newspaper or a paper bag for the cardboard, follow the directions in the Cardboard Mission section for Creating the Mission Walls, Creating the Courtyard Walls, Creating the Church Walls, and Creating the End Wall on pages 14 through 19. Once you have created the paper pattern pieces, follow the directions in the next section, Cutting Out the Walls.

The remains of this wall at Mission Santa Clara reveal the thickness of the adobe-brick walls and the layer of limestone stucco.

Cutting Out the Walls

1. Follow the recipe for modeling dough or sand clay on pages 87 through 89 to make the dough or clay.
2. Spread a sheet of waxed paper over your work area. Divide the batch of dough or clay into two or three baseball-sized pieces. Using a rolling pin, roll out each piece into a quarter-inch-thick rectangle shape on the waxed paper.
3. Place the pattern pieces on the dough as close to the edge of the dough as possible, and cut around the pieces with a dinner knife. Do not cut out the door, windows, or arches until you have completed step 4.
4. Remove the excess dough or clay from around the pieces and use a spatula to gently lift and place each wall on a cookie sheet.
5. Again, place the pattern pieces on the walls. Cut out any openings for arches on the courtyard walls—and doors or windows on the church walls—and lift the cutouts from the walls with a dinner knife.
6. If your church has a scalloped facade and you would like to place a cross on top, insert the toothpick cross (see page 82) $\frac{1}{4}$ inch into the top of the facade, positioning the cross so that it is centered.
7. To add texture to the walls, refer to Adding Texture, which follows. Then allow 24 to 48 hours for the walls to completely dry before assembling them on the base.

Adding Texture

You can easily create the appearance of adobe brick by applying pressure with a dinner knife in the still-soft dough. Gently press the length of the knife blade horizontally and then vertically into the dough or clay. A checkerboard pattern will cover each wall piece.

Assembling the Model

When the dough or clay is completely dry, use duct or packing tape to assemble and then attach the mission, courtyard, and church walls to the base. Follow the directions for Assembling the Walls and Attaching the Walls to the Base on pages 19 through 23. (The instructions give details for working with cardboard. Substitute modeling dough or sand clay walls for cardboard. The back side of your dough or clay walls is the side that dried flat against the cookie sheet.)

Finishing the Walls

You may have added red food coloring when you mixed the dough, or you may have decided to leave your modeling dough the natural color so your model would resemble the white-washed exterior of many of the California missions. Another option for a modeling dough mission is to paint it an earthen red shade to resemble adobe bricks. For specific instructions on mixing acrylic paints, go to page 68. If you used sand clay, your walls will already closely resemble the sandstone missions. We recommend that you leave the sand clay model its natural color.

After finishing the walls, the next step is to create a bell wall or bell towers. To learn how to make these, turn to Bell Walls and Bell Towers, starting on page 42.

To make your mission as colorful as La Purísima, add food coloring to your modeling dough or paint your finished mission an earthen red.

SUGAR CUBE MISSION

Building a mission from sugar cubes closely resembles the method used by Indian laborers when they constructed the original missions from adobe bricks. Because you will be assembling the sugar cubes on paper pattern pieces, this project takes a little more time than building the cardboard model, but you will end up with a sturdier mission. The sugar cube model will be heavy, so it needs the support of a quarter-inch plywood base.

YOU WILL NEED:
plywood base (quarter-inch thick) • newspaper or 1 large paper grocery bag • ruler • pencil • scissors • 4 to 6 boxes sugar cubes, all the same brand (approximately 800 to 1,000 cubes) • crayons or colored markers • white household glue

Optional materials
If you decide to create walls with openings, you will also need the following materials.
1 strip of sturdy noncorrugated or corrugated cardboard (8 x $\frac{1}{2}$ inches) • white acrylic paint • small paintbrush

Creating the Pattern Pieces

There are two ways to make doors and windows on your sugar cube mission walls. You may, as you assemble the rows, leave out sugar cubes to create actual openings for doors, windows, and bells. The other option is to use crayons or colored markers to draw those details on your finished walls. If you choose to create actual openings, follow the directions here to create pattern pieces, and then go to Assembling Walls with Openings on page 30. Keep in mind that you will not be able to create arched openings because of the cubes' straight edges.

Gluing sugar cubes to paper pattern pieces of the walls, and then gluing the walls to the plywood base, results in the sturdiest sugar cube missions. Measure, draw, and cut out pattern pieces in the following dimensions from newspaper or a paper bag.

Mission Walls

Measure, draw, and cut out one wall in each of the following dimensions. In pencil, label these pieces "mission walls."

- ▶ 18 x 3 inches
- ▶ 15 x 3 inches
- ▶ 8 x 3 inches

Courtyard Walls

Courtyard walls with cutout arches cannot be created using sugar cubes, because the many missing cubes would make the walls too weak. If you would like cutout arches on the courtyard walls, you may decide to create the courtyard walls from cardboard and paint them white to match the sugar cubes. To make cardboard courtyard walls with cutout arches, follow the directions in Creating the Courtyard Walls on page 14 and do not cut out pieces in the dimensions provided in this section. If you plan to draw arches on the courtyard walls, measure, draw, and cut out one wall in each of the following dimensions. In pencil, label these pieces "courtyard walls."

- ▶ 16 x 2½ inches
- ▶ 11 x 2½ inches
- ▶ 6 x 2½ inches

Church Walls

On most missions, the roof rests on two walls that narrow to a point or peak. On some of the missions, the roof rests on one peaked roof and leans against an elaborate scalloped facade, or front, that extends

Helpful Hint

Keep a piece of paper towel on hand to wipe up extra glue that seeps between the cubes.

Helpful Hint

To find out what we mean when we say basic peaked roof and scalloped facade, see page 16.

above the roof line. You will build the basic peaks or scalloped facade once the walls are attached to the base. The rectangular pattern pieces you are about to cut will make up the bottom four inches of the walls. Measure, draw, and cut out two walls in each of the following dimensions. In pencil, label these pieces "church walls."

▶ 9 x 4 inches
▶ 8 x 4 inches

Assembling the Walls

To construct the walls, you will glue the sugar cubes in rows onto the pattern pieces you have cut out. If you have decided to create walls with openings, skip to Assembling Walls with Openings on page 30.

1. Create the church walls first. Place the pattern piece for the church facade in front of you so that the 4-inch sides are to your left and right.
2. Apply a line of glue near the edge of the 8-inch side nearest you.
3. Starting from the left side and working to the right side, set the first cube flush against the bottom of the 8-inch side closest to you. Add another cube next to the first. Continue to add cubes, positioning them side by side on the line of glue.
4. Apply a line of glue on the pattern piece ¼ inch above the row of cubes that you just set.
5. Set the first cube flush against the left side of the pattern piece. Position the second row of cubes so it rests on the top of the first row of cubes. Continue to add cubes, positioning them side by side on the line of glue. The cubes in the second row will be aligned directly above each cube in the first row. (Figure 8)

Figure 8

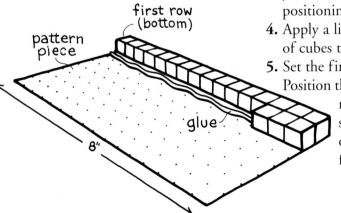

pattern piece

first row (bottom)

glue

8"

6. Repeat steps 4 and 5 until the entire pattern piece is covered with rows of sugar cubes. Approximately 15 sugar cubes will fit across an 8-inch wall and about 17 cubes will fit across a 9-inch wall. Glue cubes as close to the right-hand edge as you can without extending them beyond the edge of the pattern piece. You can trim the pattern piece later.

7. Repeat steps 1 through 6 on the other 8- x 4-inch piece to create the second peaked roof.

8. Assemble the two 9- x 4-inch church walls, all of the courtyard walls, and all of the mission walls using the same method described in this section.

9. Use crayons or colored markers to draw in doors, windows, or bell arches. Refer to pictures of the missions for ideas on where to position these features.

10. Let each wall piece dry for two hours before gluing the walls to the base. Trim any excess paper from the wall's edges.

Assembling Walls with Openings

To create your sugar cube model with actual openings for doors and windows, you will need to leave out sugar cubes as you assemble the walls on the pattern pieces and then ask an adult to use an X-acto knife to cut the paper from the back of the openings. Select one of the 8- x 4-inch church wall pattern pieces to be the front of the church.

Church Facade Wall

Look at the pictures of the California missions at the end of this book and you will see that most churches had a door in the center of the church front with a single window directly above it. Your door will be equal to the width of three sugar cubes and as tall as four cubes. To

Helpful Hint

Not all sugar "cubes" are perfect cubes. Some have one face that is larger. If this is true of your sugar cubes, be sure to assemble them so that on every wall the same size face is always in contact with the glue. It does not matter which face you decide to glue to the pattern piece.

center the door, make sure you have the same amount of cubes on each side of the door opening.

The row of sugar cubes above the door opening needs to be supported with a piece of sturdy noncorrugated or corrugated cardboard. Cardboard bridges must extend the entire length of the wall to ensure that all rows stacked above the openings are level.

1. Place the church-facade pattern piece in front of you so that the 4-inch sides are to your left and right.
2. From the lower left-hand corner, apply a 3-inch-long line of glue near the bottom of the 8-inch side nearest you.
3. Starting from the lower left-hand corner, set the first cube flush against the corner edges of the pattern piece. Set a second cube next to the first. Continue until you have glued six cubes. That should cover the glue.
4. To create an opening for the door, you now need to leave out three cubes. Place cubes 7, 8, and 9 but do not glue them down. Mark cubes 7, 8, and 9 with an X.
5. Apply a line of glue from the right side of cube 9 to the right-hand corner of the pattern piece, along the bottom. (Figure 9)

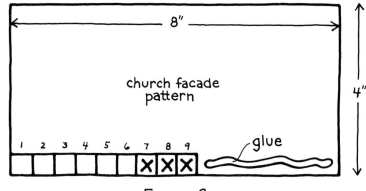

Figure 9

6. Set down cube 10 so it is glued in line with the others. Continue setting through cube 15 to cover the bottom of your pattern piece. (If there is a bit left showing to the right you can trim it later.)

7. Remove the three cubes marked with an X.

8. Apply a line of glue on the pattern piece $\frac{1}{4}$ inch above the row of cubes that you just set. Do not apply glue above the missing cubes.

9. Again, set the first cube flush against the left side of the pattern piece. Position the second row of cubes so it comes in contact with the top of the first row of cubes. Continue to add cubes, positioning them side by side on the line of glue. The cubes in the second row will be aligned directly above the cubes in the first row. When you reach the door opening, skip three cubes and continue gluing cubes until you reach the end of the pattern piece.

10. Follow steps 2 through 9 to glue two more rows.

11. Create a cardboard bridge for the fifth row of cubes, which goes over the opening.

12. Apply a thin line of glue directly to the top of the sugar cubes in the fourth row (the side that is the top of the partial wall).

13. Set the cardboard strip over the line of glue. (Figure 10)

14. Apply a line of glue on the paper pattern piece $\frac{1}{4}$ inch above the cardboard bridge.

15. Set the next row of cubes on the line of glue so one side touches the cardboard strip.

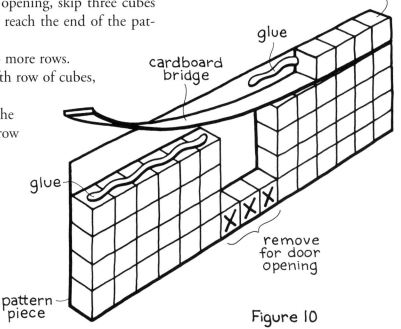

Figure 10

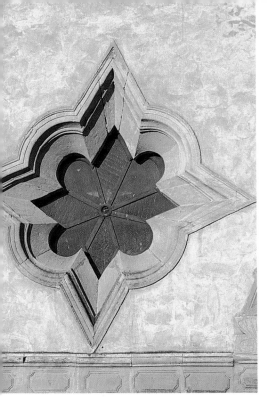

This intricate window, called the Mudéjar Star, can be seen at San Carlos Borromeo de Carmelo, also known as Mission Carmel.

16. If you want to include a window above the door, follow the instructions in Windows below. Otherwise, continue gluing rows until the whole piece is covered.

17. Trim any excess paper from the wall's edges.

Windows

Most missions had one window above the door on the church facade. Your windows will be one cube wide by two cubes tall. To make a window above the door, follow the instructions provided here.

1. Starting from the left, apply a 3¾-inch-long line (enough to glue down seven cubes) of glue ¼ inch above the last row of cubes.

2. Starting from the left side and working to the right side, set the first cube flush against the edge of the pattern piece. Add another cube next to the first. Continue to add cubes, to cover the glue until you have glued seven cubes.

3. Now you need to leave out one cube to create an opening for the window. Set cube 8 to the right of the seventh cube to mark the window opening. Use a pencil to mark an X on this cube.

4. Apply a thin line of glue from the right side of cube 8 to the right-hand edge of the pattern piece.

5. Set down cube 9 so it is glued in line with the others. Continue setting through cube 15 to complete the row.

6. Remove the one cube marked with an X to create the window opening.

7. Apply a line of glue on the pattern piece ¼ inch above the row of cubes that you just set. Do not apply glue above the missing cube.

8. Again, set the first cube flush against the left side of the pattern piece. Position the new row of cubes so it comes in contact with

the top of the last row of cubes. Continue to add cubes, positioning them side by side on the line of glue. The cubes in the new row will be aligned directly above the cubes in the last row. When you reach the window opening, skip one cube and continue gluing cubes until you reach the end of the pattern piece.

9. Apply a thin line of glue to the pattern piece ¼ inch above the row of cubes that you just set. (The glue should extend over the window opening.)

10. To complete the wall, set the next row of cubes without leaving out any cubes.

11. Assemble the other 8- x 4-inch church wall and the two 9- x 4-inch church walls. You may leave out one cube for two rows to create windows as described above. If you choose to create windows, create no more than three per 9- x 4-inch wall and no more than two per 8- x 4-inch wall. Position all windows on the same two rows of sugar cubes for the sturdiest walls.

12. Assemble the three courtyard walls and the three mission walls using the same method described in Assembling the Walls on page 19.

13. Let each wall piece dry for two hours before gluing the walls to the base. Trim any excess paper from the walls' edges.

Attaching the Walls to the Base

Attaching the sugar cube walls involves gluing the walls to the base along the placement lines you have drawn. Once the walls are attached to the base, you will build the two peaks required for a basic peaked roof, or one scallop and one peak if you have decided to create a scalloped facade. You will attach the church walls first, then the courtyard walls, and finally, the mission walls.

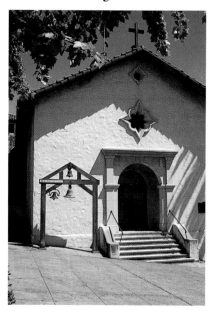

Bells may be hung throughout your courtyard from posts like this one at San Rafael Arcángel.

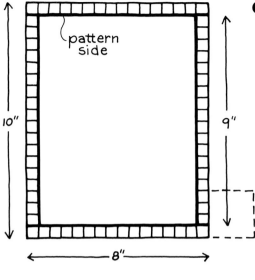

10″ **8″** **9″**

pattern
side

Figure 11

Church Walls

1. Position the plywood base in front of you so that the placement lines for the church walls are in the lower right-hand corner.
2. On the base, apply a thin line of glue to the 8-inch church-wall placement line farthest from you.
3. Set the 8- x 4-inch church wall (the wall you have decorated as the back) on the line of glue so that the paper-pattern side faces you.
4. On the base, apply a thin line of glue along the 8-inch church-wall placement line nearest you.
5. Set the front church wall on the glued placement line so that the paper-pattern side faces the first wall you set.
6. Apply a thin line of glue to the 9-inch church-wall placement line to your left.
7. Set one of the 9-inch church walls on the glued placement line so that the paper-pattern side faces the center of the church and the wall rests within the 8-inch walls.
8. Apply a thin line of glue to the remaining 9-inch church-wall placement line.
9. Set the second 9-inch church wall on the glued placement line so that the paper side faces the center of the church and the wall rests within the 8-inch walls. (Figure 11)

Courtyard Walls

1. Apply a thin line of glue along the 6-inch courtyard-wall placement line that touches the church. Set this courtyard wall on the placement line so that the paper-pattern side faces the mission-wall placement line.
2. Apply a thin line of glue along the 11-inch courtyard-wall placement line. Set this courtyard wall on the placement line so that

the paper-pattern side faces the mission-wall placement line. Make sure the right side of the wall touches the 6-inch courtyard wall.

3. Apply a thin line of glue along the 16-inch courtyard-wall placement line. Set this courtyard wall on the placement line so that the paper-pattern side faces the mission-wall placement line. Make sure the right side of the wall touches the 11-inch courtyard wall.

Mission Walls

1. Apply a thin line of glue along the 8-inch mission-wall placement line that touches the church wall. Set this mission wall on the placement line so the paper-pattern side faces the courtyard wall.

2. Apply a thin line of glue along the 15-inch mission-wall placement line. Set the 15-inch mission wall on the placement line so that the paper-pattern side faces the courtyard wall. Make sure the right side of the wall touches the 8-inch mission wall.

3. Apply a thin line of glue along the 18-inch mission-wall placement line. Set the 18-inch mission wall on the placement line so that the paper-pattern side faces the courtyard wall. Make sure the right side of the wall touches the 15-inch mission wall.

End Wall

After you have attached your walls to the base, you will need to close up the small opening between the mission walls and the courtyard walls. You will be able to fit in the opening two columns of cubes, both five cubes tall. Assemble the cubes on the base instead of on paper pattern pieces.

1. Position the base so the church is in the lower right-hand corner.

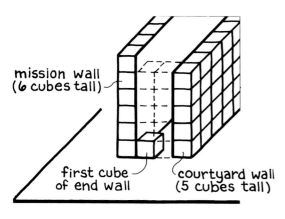

mission wall
(6 cubes tall)

first cube
of end wall

courtyard wall
(5 cubes tall)

Figure 12

2. Between the mission and courtyard walls to your left on the mission-wall placement line nearest you, apply a small drop of glue directly onto the base, to the right of the mission wall. (Figure 12)

3. Set one cube to cover the glue.

4. Apply a drop of glue to the top of the cube you just set.

5. Repeat steps 3 and 4 until you have glued a total of five cubes.

6. Apply a drop of glue directly onto the base, to the left of the courtyard wall.

7. Repeat steps 3 and 4 until you have glued a total of five cubes. The rows are one cube shorter than the mission wall to accommodate the roof you will be adding.

Preparing the Walls for the Roof

As you read in Church Walls, some mission churches had front and back peaked walls, while others had a peak in the back and an elaborate scalloped facade in the front. If you have chosen to create a basic peaked roof, follow the directions in the next section, Building the Church Peaks. If you are building a scalloped facade, finish the back wall by following the directions for Building the Church Peaks, steps 1 through 3. Then finish the front wall by following the directions for Building a Scalloped Facade on page 38.

Building the Church Peaks

On the front and back church walls, you will create roof peaks by adding four more rows of sugar cubes, for a total of 12 rows. As there is no pattern piece for the peak, you will apply the glue to the top of each row before building the next row. Each of the four rows will be shorter than the previous row.

1. On one of the 8-inch church walls, start the ninth row 1½ cubes in from the left-hand edge. Stop building the row 1½ cubes before you reach the right-hand edge of the wall. For row 10, repeat this process, indenting 1½ cubes from each edge of row 9.
2. For row 11, indent two cubes from each edge of row 10. (Row 11 will have a total of five cubes.)
3. Row 12, the final row, has only one cube. Glue the cube directly on top of the middle cube in row 11.
4. Repeat steps 1 through 3 on the other church wall to create the second peak.

Building a Scalloped Facade

Only the church front has a scalloped facade. The back wall will be peaked. To build that peak, follow steps 1 through 3 in Building the Church Peaks. Then create the front scallop by following the directions provided here. The scallop will consist of seven more rows of cubes for a total of 15 rows.

1. Skipping the first cube on the left, apply a thin line of glue along the top of row 8, stopping when you have one cube left on the right.
2. To set row 9, indent one cube from each edge of row 8.
3. Apply glue to the top of row 9, skipping the first and last cubes. To set row 10, indent one cube from each edge of row 9.
4. Glue and set rows 11 through 15, indenting one cube from each edge of the previous row. (Figure 13)

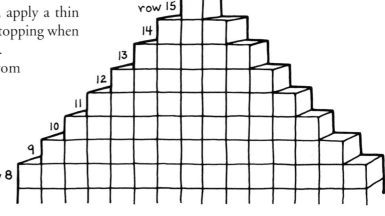

Figure 13

Finishing the Walls

To complete your mission walls, you may leave the sugar cubes their natural color. You have already used crayons or colored markers to color in doors and windows on the church walls. If you have chosen to draw arches on solid sugar cube courtyard walls, draw those now. If the cardboard bridges you have used are visible, you can paint them with white acrylic paint.

After finishing the walls, the next step is to create bells and a bell wall or bell tower. To learn how to make these, turn to the next sections.

BELLS

The chiming of bells was a constant feature of mission life. Bells called the padres and the neophytes to prayer services and meals. Some missions had one bell tower, located on either the right or left side of the church facade. A few missions had two bell towers, one on each side of the facade. Several missions did not have a bell tower but had a bell wall instead.

A bell tower or a bell wall may be created from the materials you have used to build the mission walls. A bell tower may also be made from a one-quart milk carton. Except for the sugar-cube bell tower, which requires only two bells, you will need four bells for each bell tower or bell wall. You may use purchased bells or you may make cardboard bells. Follow the directions in the next section to make bells. If you will be using purchased bells, skip to Preparing the Bells for Hanging on page 40.

With modeling dough, you can create a bell wall to resemble this example at Mission Santa Inés.

Making Cardboard Bells

YOU WILL NEED:

*corrugated cardboard (at least 6 x 2 inches) • pencil
• ruler • scissors or X-acto knife*

1. On the cardboard, draw bells that measure 1 inch tall, 1 inch wide across the base, and $^1/_2$ inch wide across the top. You will need four bells per tower or bell wall.
2. Use scissors or ask an adult to use an X-acto knife to cut out the bells.

Preparing the Bells for Hanging

The materials you will need to hang the bells will vary depending upon the type of material used to create the bell wall or bell tower. Follow the materials list and instructions for the bell wall or bell tower you plan to make.

YOU WILL NEED:

for cardboard or foam corboard bell walls
   *purchased or cardboard bells (4 per bell wall or bell tower)
   • ruler • aluminum foil (one 2-inch square per cardboard
   bell) • 4 round toothpicks*

*for sugar cube bell walls or bell towers or milk carton, cardboard,
or foam corboard bell towers*
   *purchased or cardboard bells (4 per bell wall or bell tower or 2
   per sugar cube bell tower) • ruler • white household
   glue • 3-inch pieces of string (one per bell) • aluminum
   foil (one 2-inch square per cardboard bell)*

for modeling dough or sand clay bell walls or bell towers
purchased or cardboard bells (4 per bell wall or bell tower)
• *ruler* • *white household glue* • *1 straightened small*
paper clip cut into 4 pieces, each approximately 1 inch long
• *aluminum foil (one 2-inch square per cardboard bell)*

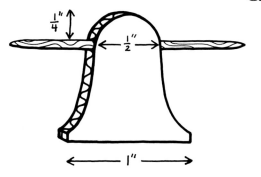

Figure 14

Cardboard or Foam Corboard Bell Wall

1. If you are using purchased bells, insert a toothpick through the top ring. If you have made cardboard bells, along the left edge of the bell, measure down ¼ inch from the top and push a toothpick sideways through the corrugation to the other edge of the bell. Adjust the toothpick so it extends equally on each side. Do this for each bell. (Figure 14)
2. Cover the bell with one of the aluminum foil squares, taking care to wrap and neatly turn the foil around the edges. Now skip to Bell Walls (page 42) or Bell Towers (page 51) to learn how to create a wall or tower in which to hang the bells.

All Other Bell Walls or Bell Towers
For purchased bells
If you are using sugar cubes, a milk carton, or creating a cardboard or foam corboard bell tower, thread one end of string through the ring at the top of the each bell and tie a double knot to secure to the ring. If you are using modeling dough or sand clay to create your bell wall or tower, or you are creating a pipe cleaner bell post, you do not have to prepare the bells in any way. Set the bells aside and go to Bell Walls on page 42 or Bell Towers on page 51 to learn how to build the bell wall or tower.

for cardboard bells

1. On one face of each bell, from the top, peel back the outside paper layer of the cardboard in the direction of the bell's base. Peel down about ¼ inch.
2. At the center top of the bell, apply a few drops of glue between the corrugation and the outside layer.
3. Press the string to the glue with the remaining string extending from the top of the bell. If you are working with modeling dough or sand clay walls, use a straightened paper clip piece instead of string.
4. Press the cardboard layers back together. (Figure 15)
5. Cover the bell with one of the aluminum foil squares, taking care to wrap and neatly turn the foil around the edges. Let the bell dry for 30 minutes before hanging. Move on to Bell Walls below or Bell Towers (page 51) to learn how to create a wall or tower in which to hang the bells.

BELL WALLS

You can create a bell wall using any of the materials you have used to build the rest of the mission. If you are building with sugar cubes, turn to Sugar Cube Bell Wall on page 48. If you will be constructing your bell wall with modeling dough or sand clay, you will first need to make a paper pattern piece. Instructions for Cardboard or Foam Corboard Bell Wall or Bell Wall Pattern Piece follow. Substitute newspaper or a paper grocery bag for the cardboard or foam corboard.

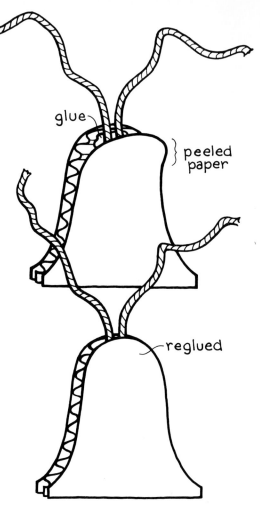

Figure 15

(Facing page) **Bellringers at San Juan Capistrano sounded the bells by pulling on ropes attached to the clappers.**

CARDBOARD OR FOAM CORBOARD BELL WALL OR BELL WALL PATTERN PIECE

If you are creating a paper pattern piece, use the instructions provided here and then turn to Modeling Dough or Sand Clay Bell Wall on page 46 for further instructions. If you are using cardboard or foam corboard to make the bell wall, use the instructions provided here to create your actual bell wall.

YOU WILL NEED:
for a cardboard or foam corboard bell wall
corrugated cardboard or foam corboard (at least 6 x 7 inches)
- *4 prepared bells, attached to toothpicks* • *pencil*
- *ruler* • *scissors or X-acto knife* • *duct or packing tape*

for a paper pattern piece
newspaper or paper grocery bag (at least 6 x 7 inches)
- *pencil* • *ruler* • *scissors*

Creating the Bell Wall or Bell Wall Pattern Piece

1. On the cardboard, foam corboard, newspaper, or paper grocery bag, measure and draw a 6- x 7-inch rectangle.
2. Place the rectangle in front of you with the 7-inch sides to your left and right.
3. Along the 6-inch side farthest from you, find the center point (3 inches) and make a dot. Label this dot A.
4. Starting from the lower right-hand corner, measure up 4 inches

along the 7-inch side and make a dot. Label this dot B.

5. Starting from the lower left-hand corner, measure up 4 inches along the 7-inch side and make a dot. Label this dot C.

6. Draw a scalloped line from dot A to dot B.

7. Draw a scalloped line from dot A to dot C.

8. Use scissors to cut out a paper pattern piece bell wall. Ask an adult to use an X-acto knife to cut out a cardboard or foam corboard bell wall.

Creating the Bell Arches

1. Place your cardboard, foam corboard, or paper pattern piece bell wall in front of you with the 7-inch sides to your left and right and the scalloped top farthest from you.

2. To draw the first two arches, from the lower left-hand corner, measure 1 inch up along the 7-inch side and make a dot. Label this dot X.

3. From the lower right-hand corner, measure 1 inch up along the 7-inch side and make a dot. Label this dot Y.

4. Use the ruler to lightly draw a straight line from dot X to dot Y.

5. From dot X, measure in 1 inch along the line and make a dot. Label this dot A.

6. From dot A, measure $1\frac{1}{2}$ inches to the right and make a second dot. Label this dot B.

7. Find the center point between dots A and B ($\frac{3}{4}$ inch) and make a small mark. From there, measure up $1\frac{1}{2}$ inches and make a third dot. Label this dot C.

8. Starting from dot A, draw an arch connecting it to dot C and then to dot B.

9. Starting from dot B, measure 1 inch to the right along the line and make a dot. Label this dot A.

The bell wall at Mission San Diego de Alcalá housed five bells and was topped with a cross.

44

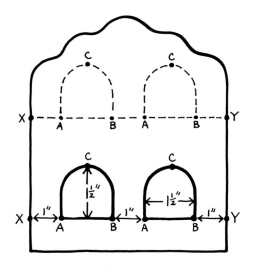

Figure 16

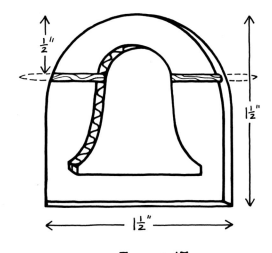

Figure 17

10. Repeat steps 6 through 8 to draw the next arch.

11. To draw the second two arches, from the lower left-hand corner of the wall, measure 4 inches up along the 7-inch side and make a dot. Label this dot X.

12. From the lower right-hand corner of the wall, measure 4 inches up along the 7-inch side and make a dot. Label this dot Y. Use a ruler to draw a straight line from dot X to dot Y.

13. Repeat steps 5 through 10 to draw the arches. (Figure 16). Use scissors or ask an adult to use an X-acto knife to cut out the arches. If you plan to use modeling clay or sand clay to make your bell wall, go to Modeling Dough or Sand Clay Bell Wall on page 46.

Hanging the Bells

1. Using purchased or cardboard bells with toothpicks already attached (from Preparing the Bells on page 40), insert one end of the toothpick into one side of the bell arch opening ½ inch from the top.

2. Push the toothpick into the side of the bell arch until you are able to insert the toothpick's other end into the other side of the arch.

3. Adjust the toothpick as needed so the bell is centered in the bell opening. (Figure 17)

Attaching the Bell Wall to the Base

1. Position the mission base so the church is in the lower right-hand corner.

2. Position the bell wall in front of you with the 7-inch sides to your left and right and the scalloped edge farthest from you. On the 6-inch edge nearest you, apply at least two 2-inch pieces of duct or packing tape vertically, extending 1 inch below the cardboard.

3. Position the bell wall on top of the mission-wall placement line nearest you, to the left of the church. The taped side of the bell wall should face the courtyard.

4. Firmly press the tape to the base.

MODELING DOUGH OR SAND CLAY BELL WALL

YOU WILL NEED:

¹/₄ batch modeling dough or sand clay • 1 bell wall pattern piece • waxed paper • rolling pin • dinner knife • spatula • cookie sheet

1. Spread a sheet of waxed paper over your work area. Form the dough or clay into a ball. Using a rolling pin, roll out the piece into a quarter-inch-thick rectangle shape on the waxed paper.

2. Place the paper pattern piece on top of the dough or clay, and cut around the pattern with a dinner knife. Do not cut out the bell openings until you have completed step 3.

3. Use a spatula to gently lift and place each wall on a cookie sheet.

4. Again, place the paper pattern piece on the wall. Cut out the arches and lift the arch cutouts from the wall with a dinner knife.

Inserting a Hook to Hang the Bells

If you have purchased bells to hang in your tower or bell wall, it is best to insert a hook in the dough or clay while it is still soft. If you will be

Helpful Hint

Don't forget to erase the pencil markings from the bell wall.

hanging cardboard bells, follow the directions to make the bells in Making Cardboard Bells and Preparing the Bells for Hanging both on page 40. Then skip to step 3.

YOU WILL NEED:
2 small paper clips (for purchased bells) • *4 purchased bells (³/₄ inch) or 4 cardboard bells*

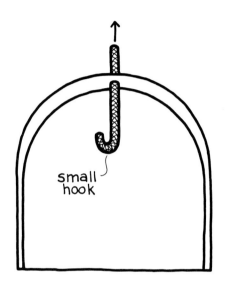

small hook

Figure 18

1. Straighten out each paper clip and cut each one with sharp scissors or garden shears into two or three 1-inch pieces. You will need one of these pieces per bell.
2. Have an adult bend a small hook at one end of each piece of wire.
3. From inside the opening, insert the straight end of the wire into the center of the top of the arch. (Figure 18)
4. If you are using purchased bells, hang them from the hooks after you have attached the walls to the base.
5. If you want to create the appearance of adobe brick on your dough or clay bell wall, turn to Adding Texture on page 25. Allow 24 to 48 hours for the bell wall to dry before attaching the wall to the base.

Inserting a Cross on Top of the Bell Wall

Many bell walls had a cross centered on the top. If you would like to insert a cross into the top of your bell wall, do the following:
1. Follow the instructions for Small Crosses on page 83 to create the cross.
2. Insert the cross ¹/₄ inch into the top edge of the bell wall, positioning the cross in the center.

Attaching the Bell Wall to the Base

1. When the bell wall is dry, position the base in front of you so that the placement lines for the church are in the lower right-hand corner.
2. Apply a thin line of glue along the 6-inch line to the left of the church.
3. Place the modeling dough or sand clay bell wall on the glue. Hold for five minutes to allow the glue to set.

SUGAR CUBE BELL WALL

As you did when you built the other sugar cube walls, create a paper pattern piece and then glue the cubes to the pattern.

YOU WILL NEED:
¹/₂ box sugar cubes (approximately 100 cubes of the original 800 to 1,000) • white household glue • scissors • X-acto knife • 4 purchased bells (³/₄ inch) or 4 cardboard bells, prepared for hanging

Creating the Bell Wall Pattern Piece

YOU WILL NEED:
newspaper or paper grocery bag (at least 5 x 7 inches) • pencil • ruler • scissors

1. On newspaper or paper grocery bag, measure and draw a 5- x 7-inch rectangle.
2. Place the rectangle in front of you with the 7-inch sides to your left and right.

San Juan Bautista's bell wall had three openings. Your sugar cube wall will have four.

3. Along the 5-inch side farthest from you, find the center point (2$\frac{1}{2}$ inches) and make a dot. Label this dot A.

4. Starting from the lower right-hand corner, measure up 4 inches along the 7-inch side and make a dot. Label this dot B.

5. Starting from the lower left-hand corner, measure up 4 inches along the 7-inch side and make a dot. Label this dot C. With a ruler, draw a straight line from dot A to dot B and from dot A to dot C.

6. Use scissors to cut out the paper-pattern piece bell wall.

Assembling the Bell Wall

1. Place the pattern piece in front of you with the 4-inch sides to your left and right and the peak farthest from you. Along the 5-inch side closest to you, apply a thin line of glue $\frac{1}{4}$ inch up from the bottom.

2. Glue three rows of cubes that are each 10 cubes long.

3. Starting on the left-hand side, assemble rows 4 and 5 in the following manner: Glue one sugar cube, leave a space the size of two cubes, glue one cube, leave a space the size of two cubes, glue one cube, leave a space the size of two cubes, glue one cube.

4. To begin row 6, glue two cubes. Apply a drop of glue to the right-hand side of the second cube—the side that the next sugar cube will eventually touch. Do not lay down the third cube.

5. To hang the bell, press the string to the glued side of the second sugar cube so that the top of the bell almost touches the bottom of the cubes in the sixth row (the row you have just begun laying), and the bell fits into the bell opening. Extend the excess string over the top of the cubes in the sixth row.

6. Glue the third cube so that the string is sandwiched between two cubes. (Figure 19)

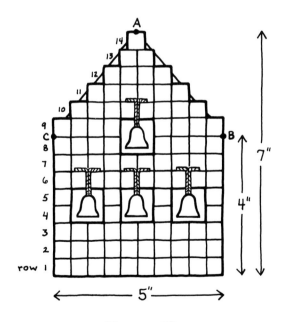

Figure 19

7. Glue the next two cubes. Now your row has five cubes.

8. Use the same method that you used in steps 5 through 7 to hang the second bell. You will sandwich the string between the fifth and sixth cubes.

9. Glue cubes 7 and 8.

10. Use the same method that you used in steps 5 through 7 to hang the third bell. You will sandwich the string between the eighth and ninth cubes.

11. Glue the tenth cube to finish row 6.

12. In row 7, glue 10 cubes.

13. To assemble rows 8 and 9, glue four cubes, leave a space the size of two cubes, glue four cubes.

14. Assemble row 10 and hang the fourth bell. From the left-hand edge, indent by the width of one cube. Glue four cubes.

15. Insert a bell and glue one cube. Glue three more cubes. You will end row 10 one cube in from the right-hand edge.

16. To complete rows 11 through 13, from each edge, indent the width of one cube. Start row 11 one cube to the right of where row 10 began. End it one cube to the left of where row 10 ended. Continue assembling rows and indenting one cube from each side. Row 14 will have just one centered cube.

17. Allow one hour for the wall to dry.

18. Use scissors or ask an adult to use an X-acto knife to cut extra paper from the edges and from the bell openings. Be careful not to cut the bells or the strings.

Attaching the Bell Wall to the Base

1. Position the base in front of you so that the church is in the lower right-hand corner.

Modeled after the Great Stone Church at San Juan Capistrano, the church at Mission San Luis Rey de Francia was shaped like a cross and could hold 1,000 worshipers.

2. Apply a thin line of glue along the 6-inch placement line to the left of the church.
3. Set the bell wall on the line of glue so that the paper pattern side faces the center of the base.

BELL TOWERS

A bell tower may be created from the materials you have used to build the mission walls or from a one-quart milk carton. Refer to the pictures of missions in this book for bell tower ideas. Notice that some missions have two bell towers and others have one. Bell towers have individual styles. Bell towers may be single- or double-tiered, and they may have a dome or pyramid top. Decide how many and what style bell towers you would like to create and follow the directions provided here to build them. If you are using sugar cubes to build the bell tower, go to Sugar Cube Bell Tower on page 60. To create a bell tower from any other material, follow the instructions in the next section.

CARDBOARD OR FOAM CORBOARD BELL TOWER OR BELL TOWER PATTERN PIECE

If you are using modeling dough or sand clay to make the bell tower, use the instructions provided here to create a pattern piece on newspaper or a paper grocery bag. Then turn to Modeling Dough or Sand Clay Bell Tower on page 59 for further instructions. If you are using cardboard or foam corboard, use the instructions provided here to create your actual bell tower walls. As with the rest of the mission's wall pieces, you may either color in bell openings or cut them out.

Creating the Bell Tower
or Bell Tower Pattern Pieces

If you plan to create two cardboard or foam corboard bell towers, cut out enough pieces for both towers.

1. On the cardboard or foam corboard, measure, draw, and cut out four wall pieces $9^1/_2$ x 2 inches. If you are making your bell tower from modeling dough or sand clay, on newspaper or paper grocery bag, measure and draw one wall piece $9^1/_2$ x 2 inches.

2. On cardboard or foam corboard, measure, draw, and cut out one $2^1/_4$-inch square. Set this piece aside. Always use cardboard or foam corboard for this step, even if you are creating paper pattern pieces. If you have chosen to do a single-tiered tower, skip to Creating the Bell Arches below.

3. If you have chosen to do a double-tiered bell tower, on cardboard or foam corboard, measure and draw four wall pieces 2 x $1^1/_2$ inches. Also, measure and draw a $1^3/_4$-inch square. Set these pieces aside. Regardless of what material you use for the first tier, your second tier must be made with cardboard or foam corboard.

Creating the Bell Arches

If you plan to cut out the arches, follow the steps provided here to measure, draw, and cut out one arch on one of the walls. Then trace the arch on to the other three walls. If you plan to color in the arches, follow steps 1 through 8 to draw an arch on each of the $9^1/_2$-inch tower walls. The bell arches will be $1^1/_4$ inches wide by $1^1/_4$ inches tall. If you are creating a paper pattern piece, use these instructions to make a cutout arch on your pattern piece.

YOU WILL NEED:

for a cardboard or foam corboard bell tower
- *corrugated cardboard or foam corboard*
- *pencil*
- *ruler*
- *scissors or X-acto knife*
- *duct or packing tape*

for a paper pattern piece
- *newspaper or paper grocery bag*
- *pencil*
- *ruler*
- *scissors*

1. Position one 9¹/₂-inch wall piece in front of you with the 9¹/₂-inch sides to your left and right.
2. From the lower left-hand corner, measure 7 inches up the 9¹/₂-inch side and make a dot. Label this dot X.
3. From the lower right-hand corner, measure 7 inches up the 9¹/₂-inch side and make a dot. Label this dot Y.
4. Use a ruler to draw a straight line from dot X to dot Y.
5. From dot X, measure in ³/₈ inch along the line and make a dot. Label this dot A.
6. From dot A, measure 1¹/₄ inches to the right and make a dot. Label this dot B.
7. Find the center point between dots A and B (⁵/₈ inch) and make a small mark. From there, measure up 1¹/₄ inches and make a third dot. Label this dot C.
8. Starting from dot A, draw an arch connecting it to dot C and then to dot B.
9. For the colored arches option, repeat steps 1 through 8 on the other three walls. Then color in the arches and skip to Assembling the Bell Tower on page 54. If you have chosen to cut out the arches, use scissors or ask an adult to use an X-acto knife to cut them out. If you are creating a paper pattern piece, use scissors to cut out the arch and then go to Modeling Dough or Sand Clay Bell Tower on page 59.

Figure 20

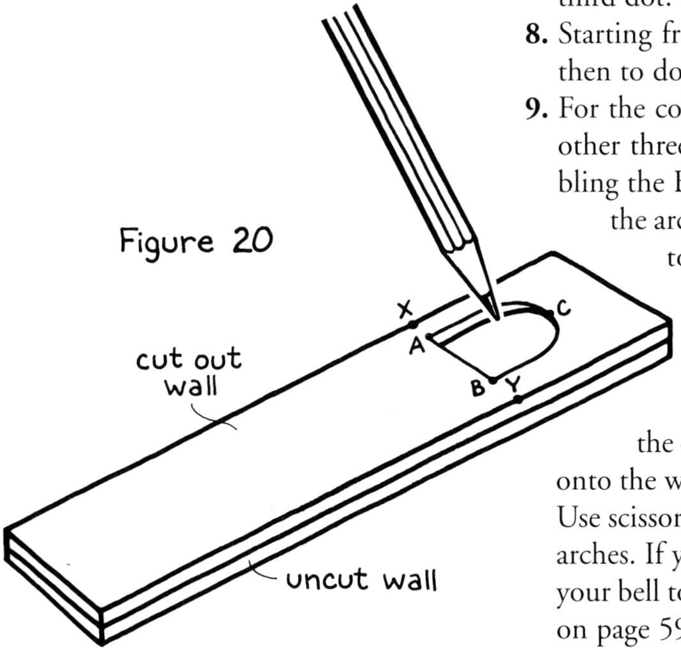

cut out wall

uncut wall

10. Place the cutout arch wall directly over one of the other 9¹/₂- x 2-inch walls. Use a pencil to trace the arch onto the wall. (Figure 20) Repeat with the two remaining walls. Use scissors or ask an adult to use an X-acto knife to cut out the arches. If you plan to use modeling dough or sand clay to make your bell tower, go to Modeling Dough or Sand Clay Bell Tower on page 59.

Assembling the Bell Tower Walls

1. With the 2-inch archless edges nearest you, lay the four bell tower walls in front of you so the 9½-inch sides touch. If you are using cardboard and one side is printed, place the pieces printed-side up. If you colored in the arches instead of cutting them out, place the side you have colored down. (Figure 21)

2. Starting ½ inch in from the edge of the left-hand wall piece, apply horizontally at even intervals two or three 7½-inch pieces of duct tape to connect all four wall pieces. (Do not cover cutout arches with tape.) Extend the tape pieces 1 inch beyond the edge of the wall piece on the right.

3. With the taped edges inside and the extended tape pieces tucked in, fold the walls at the taped joints to create a box.

4. To secure the pieces of tape nearest each of the box's ends, reach your fingers inside and press down the tape.

5. To secure the middle piece of tape inside the narrow tower, use a pencil to reach down into the box and press the piece against the tower wall.

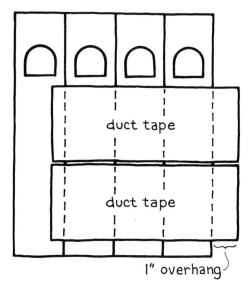

Figure 21

Attaching the Bell Tower to the Base

1. It is easiest to secure the bell tower to the base at this time. Cut a 1½-inch-long piece of duct tape in half lengthwise. On the outside of the tower, apply the piece of duct tape vertically to the bottom (farthest from the arches) of a bell tower wall. Make sure the tape extends 1 inch beyond the bottom of the tower.

2. Apply a thin line of glue to the tower placement line. Position the tower over the glued placement lines on the base, with the taped wall against the church wall.

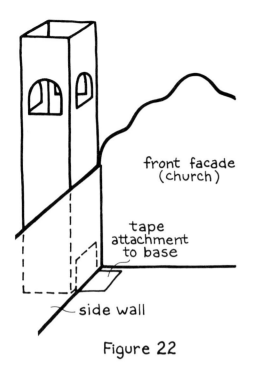

front facade
(church)

tape
attachment
to base

side wall

Figure 22

3. Slide the tape extension under the church wall and press it to the base. (Figure 22)

Attaching the Tower Roof

1. To attach the roof, apply a line of glue along the top edge of the tower's four walls.

2. Center the $2\frac{1}{4}$-inch square over the tower and press down. If you are creating a double-tiered tower, go to Creating and Attaching the Second Tier (below). If you are making a single-tiered tower, turn to Tower Tops (page 63) to finish the bell tower.

Creating and Attaching the Second Tier

1. If you have chosen to build a second bell-tower tier, lay the four 2- x $1\frac{1}{2}$-inch walls in front of you so the $1\frac{1}{2}$-inch edges are nearest you and the 2-inch sides touch. If you are using cardboard and one side is printed, place the pieces printed-side up. Cut a 6-inch piece of duct tape in half lengthwise. (You will only use one of the halves.) Starting 1 inch in from the edge of the left-hand wall piece, apply the tape horizontally to connect all four pieces. Extend the tape 1 inch beyond the edge of the wall piece on the right.

2. With the taped edges inside and the extended tape piece tucked in, fold the walls at the taped joints to create a box. Reach inside and press the tape down.

3. Apply a thin line of glue to one edge of the second tier's walls.

4. Center the glued edge on top of the tower's first-tier roof. Press down to secure.

5. To attach the roof, apply a thin line of glue along the top edge of the second tier's four walls. Position the 1¾-inch square over the second tier (align it so it meets the edges of the walls) and lightly press down to secure it to the glue.
6. Turn to Tower Tops on page 63 to learn how to finish the bell tower.

MILK CARTON BELL TOWER

A fun and easy way to make a bell tower is to use a one-quart milk carton. If you decide to make two towers, you will need two milk cartons. Follow the directions provided here for each carton.

YOU WILL NEED:

1 or 2 one-quart milk cartons (cleaned and dried, top open) • *brown paper grocery bag (brown because it will show)* • *pencil* • *ruler* • *scissors or X-acto knife* • *white household glue* • *4 purchased bells (¾ inch) or 4 cardboard bells, prepared for hanging* • *transparent tape* • *stapler* • *paper clips*

Covering the Carton

1. Measure, draw, and cut out one 11-inch square from the paper bag.
2. Apply a thin layer of glue to one side of the milk carton. Align one side of the paper square with the left-hand edge of the carton's glued side. (If one side of the paper bag is printed, make sure the printed side faces the carton.) Press the paper against the carton to secure. (Figure 23)
3. Rotate the carton so that the side you just papered is on the left.

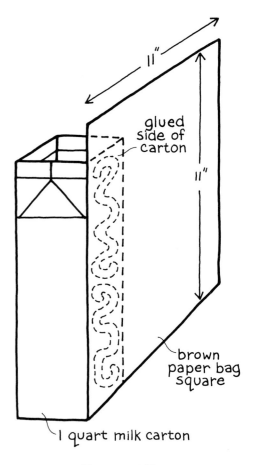

glued side of carton

brown paper bag square

1 quart milk carton

Figure 23

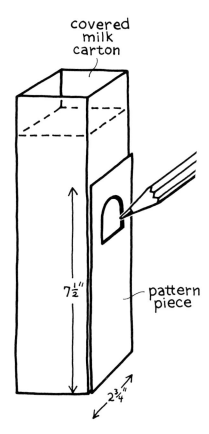

covered
milk
carton

$7\frac{1}{2}''$

pattern
piece

$2\frac{3}{4}''$

Figure 24

4. Apply glue to the side of the carton now facing you. Bring the paper around the carton's edge and smooth it over the freshly glued side.

5. Repeat steps 3 and 4 to apply paper to the carton's remaining two sides. Leave the top of the carton open—you will have to reach in the top to hang the bells later.

Creating the Bell Arches

1. On the remainder of the brown paper bag, measure, draw, and cut out a pattern piece $7\frac{1}{2}$ x $2\frac{3}{4}$ inches. Place the pattern piece in front of you with the $7\frac{1}{2}$-inch sides to your left and right.

2. From the lower left-hand corner, measure 5 inches up the $7\frac{1}{2}$-inch side and make a dot. Label this dot X.

3. From the lower right-hand corner, measure 5 inches up the $7\frac{1}{2}$-inch side and make a dot. Label this dot Y.

4. Use a ruler to draw a straight line from dot X to dot Y.

5. From dot X, measure in $\frac{5}{8}$ inch along the line and make a dot. Label this dot A.

6. From dot A, measure $1\frac{1}{2}$ inches to the right and make a dot. Label this dot B.

7. Find the center point between dots A and B ($\frac{5}{16}$ inch) and make a small mark. From there, measure up $1\frac{1}{2}$ inches and make a third dot. Label this dot C.

8. Starting from dot A draw an arch connecting it to dot C and then to dot B.

9. Use scissors to cut out the arch.

10. Hold the pattern piece against one of the carton's sides with the arch closest to the top. (Figure 24)

11. Use a pencil to trace the outline of the arch onto the carton.

12. Repeat steps 10 and 11 on each of the carton's remaining sides.

13. If you have chosen to color in the arches, do so now. If you have chosen to cut out the arches, ask an adult to cut them out using an X-acto knife.

Hanging the Bells

1. Apply a $1\frac{1}{2}$-inch piece of transparent tape horizontally across the string, $\frac{1}{2}$ inch above the bell.

2. Reaching into the top of the carton, hold the bell in front of one of the arches. Make sure that the bell hangs in the center of the arch. Tape the bell to the carton's inside wall, above the arch. Hang the other three bells.

3. When you have hung all four bells, close and staple the top of the carton to create a peaked roof. Pull together the remaining brown paper, tucking it to fit the shape of the carton top.

4. Apply a thin line of glue to one side of the carton's peak (along the very top of the carton that you just stapled shut in step 3). Neatly fold down the paper that extends above the carton to cover the glue.

5. Hold the paper to the peak with paper clips. Remove the paper clips after 30 minutes. Trim any excess paper from the peak. To create a more colorful roof, you may use red acrylic paint to color the carton's peak.

Attaching the Bell Tower to the Base

1. Position the base in front of you so that the church is in the lower right-hand corner.

2. To attach the milk carton bell tower to the base, apply a thin layer of glue to the bottom of the carton.

A full moon rises above the matching bell towers of Santa Bárbara's church.

3. Position the bell tower to the right of the church or along the mission-wall placement line to the left of the church, between the church and the courtyard walls. Press down on the carton to secure it to the base.

MODELING DOUGH OR SAND CLAY BELL TOWER

YOU WILL NEED:

1 to 2 batches modeling dough or sand clay • rolling pin • waxed paper • 1 bell tower wall pattern piece • dinner knife • cookie sheet • spatula • 4 purchased bells or 4 cardboard bells per bell tower, prepared for hanging • 1 or 2 small paper clips (only if using purchased bells) • ruler • garden shears • white household glue • duct tape

Cutting Out the Bell Tower Walls

1. Roll out the dough or clay onto your covered work surface, place the pattern piece on the dough, and use a dinner knife to cut around the pattern. If you need to review the method of cutting out dough or clay walls, turn to steps 1 through 3 in Cutting Out the Walls on page 25. Do not cut out the bell arches until you have completed steps 2 and 3 listed below.

2. Move the paper pattern piece over onto a patch of uncut dough and cut around the pattern piece. Repeat this step two more times until you have cut out a total of four pieces.

3. Remove the excess dough or clay from around the pieces and use a spatula to gently lift and place each wall onto a cookie sheet.

4. Again, place the pattern piece on one of the walls. Cut out the arched openings and lift the cutout from the wall with a dinner knife. Do this for the other three walls.

5. Follow the instructions for Inserting a Hook to Hang the Bells on page 46.

6. If you want to create the appearance of adobe brick on your dough or clay walls, turn to Adding Texture on page 25.

7. Allow 24 to 48 hours for the bell tower pieces to dry before assembling the bell tower and attaching it to the base. If pieces of the wall break off, use glue to reattach them and allow one hour for glued pieces to dry.

8. To assemble your bell tower and attach it to the base, follow the three sets of instructions on pages 54 and 55 from Assembling the Bell Tower Walls through Attaching the Tower Roof.

SUGAR CUBE BELL TOWER

If your mission is made of sugar cubes, you may make the bell tower walls of sugar cubes. However, you will need to use cardboard to top the tower and build the optional second tier. Because each of the sugar cube walls is 1/2-inch thick, you will create two 2-inch-wide sugar cube bell tower walls and two 1-inch-wide walls so the tower fits within the bell-tower placement lines. The 1-inch-wide tower walls are too small to support a bell opening, so your sugar cube bell tower will have two bells instead of four.

Creating the Walls

1. Measure, draw, and cut out of newspaper or a grocery bag two 9 1/2- x 2-inch pattern pieces and two 9 1/2- x 1-inch pattern pieces.

for single-tiered tower
- *1 box sugar cubes (about 150 of the original 800)*
- *newspaper or paper grocery bag*
- *ruler*
- *pencil*
- *scissors*
- *white household glue*
- *2 purchased or cardboard bells, prepared for hanging*
- *2 1/4-inch square of cardboard or foam corboard*

for a second tier
- *cardboard or foam corboard for four 2 x 1 1/2-inch walls*
- *1 3/4-inch square of cardboard or foam corboard*
- *white acrylic paint (for cardboard only)*
- *small paintbrush*

The mission buildings were the center of large farms, where Indian laborers were the main workforce. They plowed, sowed, and harvested crops for no pay.

2. Position one of the 9½- x 2-inch pattern pieces in front of you with the 9½-inch sides to your left and right.

3. Starting from the lower left-hand corner, glue 15 rows of cubes. If you need to review the technique to glue the sugar cubes onto the paper pattern, turn back to page 29. Although the steps listed there are for a wall of a different size, steps 2 through 5 should remind you of the important points.

4. To leave a bell opening near the top of the two 9½- x 2-inch tower walls, complete rows 16 and 17 as follows: glue one cube, leave a space the size of two cubes, and glue the last cube in the row.

5. To begin row 18 and hang the bell, glue two cubes. Apply a drop of glue to the right-hand side of the second cube—the side that the next sugar cube will eventually touch. Do not lay down the third cube.

6. To hang the bell, press the string to the glued side of the second sugar cube, so that the top of the bell almost touches the bottom of the cubes in row 18 (the row you have just begun laying) and the bell fits into the bell opening. Extend the excess string over the top of the cubes in row 18.

7. Glue the third cube so the string is in between two cubes.

8. Glue the fourth cube to finish the row. Then glue row 19.

9. Follow steps 2 through 8 to complete the other 9½- x 2-inch wall.

10. Position one of the 9½- x 1-inch pattern pieces in front of you with the 9½-inch sides to your left and right.

11. Starting from the lower left-hand corner, glue 19 rows of cubes to complete the wall.

12. Repeat steps 10 and 11 to create the other 9½- x 1-inch wall.

13. Cut out of cardboard or foam corboard one 2¼-inch square. If you have decided to build a single-tiered bell tower, skip to step 15. If you are making a double-tiered tower, create the pieces for

the second tier by following step 3 in Creating the Bell Tower or Bell Tower Pattern Pieces on page 52.

14. If you are using cardboard, use white acrylic paint to color the second tier to match the sugar cube tower.

15. Allow one to two hours for the walls to dry before attaching the bell tower to the base.

Attaching the Bell Tower to the Base

1. Position the base so the church is in the lower right-hand corner.

2. Apply a thin line of glue to the bell-tower placement lines.

3. Set one of the $9^1/_2$- x 2-inch pieces on the line farthest from you so that the paper side faces you.

4. Set one of the $9^1/_2$- x 1-inch walls on the placement line to the right, so the side of the wall butts up to the back (paper) side of the first wall you set. The paper side will face the center of the bell tower. Set the other $9^1/_2$- x 1-inch wall on the placement line to the left, so its cubed face touches the church, and its side butts up to the back of the first wall.

5. Set the other $9^1/_2$- x 2-inch piece on the line closest to you so that the paper side faces the center of the bell tower and it completely closes off the opening.

Attaching the Bell Tower Roof

1. Apply a thin line of glue along the top edge of the bell tower.

2. Center and glue the $2^1/_4$-inch cardboard or foam corboard square onto the top of the tower. If you are creating a single-tiered

San Carlos Borromeo is the only mission that still has its original bell-tower dome.

tower, skip to Tower Tops (below). If you are making a double-tiered tower, go to Creating and Attaching the Second Tier on page 55.

TOWER TOPS

Some California mission bell towers were topped with a small dome. Others had a pyramid. Refer to the pictures of the missions throughout this book to see what type of top you'd like for your bell tower.

DOME TOP

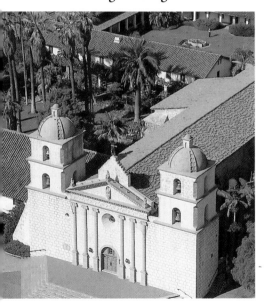

Repeated restoration efforts reconstructed Santa Bárbara's bell towers with domed tops that were not part of the original design.

The size of your dome top depends on how many tiers you made in your bell tower. Using one of the egg cups from a paper or a Styrofoam egg carton, you can make a large dome or small dome. To create a dome large enough to top a single-tiered tower, you will need to papier-mâché an egg-carton cup to increase its size. If you made a single-tiered tower, refer to the papier-mâché recipe and instructions in Exterior Treatments on page 65 through 68 to learn how to make and apply papier-mâché paste.

YOU WILL NEED:
1 egg-carton cup • scissors • ruler • white household glue

for a single-tiered tower
1 batch papier-mâché paste • strips of newspaper

1. Cut out one of the egg cups from an egg carton. If you are topping a double-tiered tower, trim ¼ inch off the wide edge of the cup (make sure the edge is even) and skip to step 4. If you are topping a single-tiered tower, go to step 2.

2. Papier-mâché the entire egg cup to increase the size of the dome. Let the papier-mâché dry overnight.

3. Trim the bottom of the dome to create an even edge.

4. Apply glue along the dome's bottom edge and press it gently to the center of the bell tower's top.

PYRAMID TOP

YOU WILL NEED:

noncorrugated cardboard (thin gauge) • pencil • ruler • transparent tape • scissors • white household glue

1. To create a top for a single-tiered tower, measure and draw one 1³/₄- x 5-inch rectangle on noncorrugated cardboard (double-tiered tower needs one 1¹/₄- x 3³/₄-inch rectangle).

2. Position the rectangle vertically in front of you so that the longer sides are on your left and right.

3. At the top left-hand corner, make a dot and label it C.

4. From dot C, measure toward you along the left side 2 inches (1¹/₂ inches for double-tiered top), make a dot, and label it E. From dot E, measure toward you another 2 inches (1¹/₂ inches for double-tiered top), make a dot, and label it G.

5. From the top right-hand corner, measure toward you along the right side 1 inch (³/₄ inch for double-tiered top), make a dot, and label it D. From dot D, measure toward you another 2 inches (1¹/₂ inches for double-tiered top), make a dot, and label it F. Label the lower right-hand corner H.

6. Starting at dot C, draw a straight line to dot D. Also connect dot D to dot E, dot E to dot F, dot F to dot G, and dot G to dot H. Label each diagonal line A and each outer edge B. (Figure 25A)

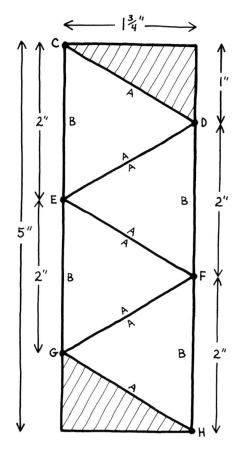

Figure 25A

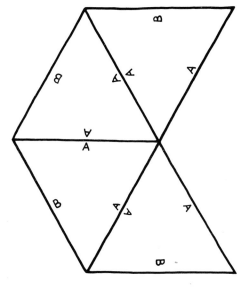

Figure 25 B

7. Cut along all lines labeled A and B, creating four equilateral triangles with 2-inch sides. (A double-tiered top will have 1½-inch sides.) Discard the two small end pieces.

8. Align the four triangles labeled-side up so all A sides meet. (Figure 25B). Apply a 1¾-inch piece of transparent tape (a 1¼-inch piece for a double-tiered tower) to cover each of the seams where A sides meet.

9. Apply a 1¾-inch piece of transparent tape (a 1¼-inch piece for a double-tiered tower) to either one of the two A sides that is not yet taped so the tape extends beyond the cardboard by ½ inch.

10. Turn the pieces over and gently push on each of the B sides. The triangles will rise up to form a pyramid. Tuck the tape extensions inside the pyramid and then secure the remaining A edges.

11. On the inside of each of the pyramid's four sides, apply a 1½-inch piece of tape vertically so the tape extends beyond the cardboard by about 1 inch. Align the bottom of each of the pyramid sides with the top of the bell tower wall.

12. Attach the pyramid's tape extensions to the tower top. Tucking the pieces of tape inside the pyramid, set the remaining two sides on the tower top. Press down gently on the pyramid to secure it.

EXTERIOR TREATMENTS

Most of the California missions were built of adobe bricks made from adobe clay, straw, and manure. San Juan Capistrano, Santa Bárbara, and San Carlos Borromeo de Carmelo, however, were built of sandstone bricks cut from nearby cliffs. Both adobe and sandstone dissolved in the rain. To protect the buildings, laborers waterproofed the exterior walls with lime stucco—a mixture of limestone, ground seashells, and water. Your exterior treatment options will vary depending on the type of material you used to create your mission. Find the material you used and choose a treatment to finish your walls.

For cardboard missions you may
- ▶ leave your mission its natural tan color
- ▶ paint it with acrylic paints
- ▶ use crayons or colored markers
- ▶ papier-mâché and then paint it (so the newsprint doesn't show)

For foam corboard missions you may
- ▶ leave your mission its natural color
- ▶ paint it with acrylic paints
- ▶ use crayons or colored markers

For modeling dough or sand clay missions you may
- ▶ leave your mission its white, tan, or red color
- ▶ paint it with acrylic paints (modeling dough only)

For sugar cube missions you may
- ▶ leave your mission its natural white color
- ▶ use crayons or colored markers

PAPIER-MÂCHÉ

Papier-mâché will give your model a texture similar to the whitewashed adobe brick of the California missions. *Papier-mâché* means "mashed paper" in French. Torn strips of paper are mixed with a paste and then applied over the surface of an object. The length of the paper strips will depend on the size of the object you are covering. Use longer strips for bigger pieces and shorter strips for smaller ones.

When the paste is dry, you can cover the papier-mâché with acrylic paint. Make the paste just before you are ready to begin applying the strips of paper to the model.

Covering your mission with papier-mâché will create a look similar to the appearance of Mission San Miguel.

YOU WILL NEED:

newspaper or scrap paper, torn into ³/₄- to 1-inch-wide strips • medium-sized mixing bowl (pottery or plastic) • large spoon (wooden or metal) • measuring cups (¹/₄ cup, ¹/₂ cup)

Ingredients:
¹/₂ cup flour • ¹/₄ to ³/₄ cup water

Because papier-mâché uses a water-based paste, this can be a messy job. Waterproof your work surface before you begin. Cover at least a two-foot-square area with two layers of old newspaper, then spread a plastic garbage bag over the paper.

Making the Paste

1. Pour the flour in the bowl, adding water a little at a time and stirring after each addition.
2. Stir the mixture until it is smooth and somewhat thick. Work out as many lumps or air bubbles as you can.

Applying the Papier-Mâché

Apply papier-mâché after you have attached all of the walls—including the optional bell wall or bell towers—to the base, but before you have attached the roofs.

1. Dip the strips, one at a time, into the paste, coating thoroughly.
2. Over the bowl, run the strip between two fingers to remove excess paste.
3. Apply the strips vertically, overlapping them, and running them outward onto the base to reinforce the walls' attachment. Work

around door, window, or bell openings. Cover your entire mission form. (Figure 26)

4. Allow 24 to 36 hours for the papier-mâché to dry, and then paint. The overlapped strips and a paste bump here and there will give your model an uneven surface resembling the texture of the adobe missions.

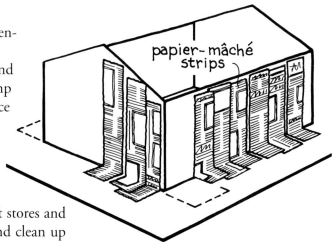

Figure 26

PAINT

Acrylic paints, sold in 2-ounce bottles, are available at craft stores and come in a variety of colors. These paints are easy to use and clean up with water. You may need to apply more than one coat of paint to cover the original color of your model. Allow the paint to dry for about one hour before applying a second coat. Use a small craft paintbrush to paint in smaller spaces and add tiny details. Use a medium-size craft paintbrush to paint entire walls.

You can buy many colors of acrylic paint, or you may create just the shades you need by combining small amounts of two colors in an aluminum pie pan or disposable plastic container.

Mixing Paints

You will be able to create all of the colors you need from yellow, red, blue, black, brown, and white. Mix equal amounts of yellow and blue to make green, red and yellow to make orange, or blue and red to make purple. Lighten any of the colors by adding small amounts of white. For example, to make tan for the mission's walls, mix some white paint with brown until you have the desired shade. White may also be added to blue paint to create a pale blue for the water fountain or trough. Darken any of the colors by adding small amounts of black.

ROOFS

Mission architecture made extensive use of red clay tile roofs. Tile roofs became an important feature of mission construction and appearance in the 1780s. The clay tiles kept out the rain, and the wide overhanging roofs protected the adobe walls from moisture.

Laborers formed clay slabs into rectangles approximately 22 inches long and from 12 inches to 20 inches wide. Then they patted the damp rectangles over curved wooden forms and left them to dry in the sun. When the clay was dry, the workers removed the rectangles from the forms and baked them in an oven called a kiln.

Your model's church and three courtyard buildings will need roofs. Using noodles or modeling clay, you can make a variety of textured roofs with a corrugated or noncorrugated cardboard base. You may also add texture to a corrugated cardboard roof by simply exposing the corrugated waves. For each of the roof styles mentioned here, you will first need to make the cardboard roof base according to the instructions in Creating the Roof Bases. Then choose a type of texturing and follow the set of instructions in Adding Texture beginning on page 72.

Creating the Roof Bases

YOU WILL NEED:

- *corrugated or noncorrugated cardboard*
- *pencil*
- *ruler*
- *scissors or X-acto knife*
- *duct or packing tape*

CHURCH ROOF

The roof base for the church will be slightly smaller if your church has a scalloped facade.

1. If you are creating a roof base for a church with a basic peaked roof, measure and draw on cardboard a 10- x 12-inch rectangle. If you are creating a roof base for a church with a scalloped facade, measure and draw on cardboard a 10- x 11-inch rectangle. If you plan to make the corrugated cardboard textured roof, draw the rectangle on the cardboard so the lines of corrugation

run in the same direction as the 10-inch lines. Use scissors or ask an adult to use an X-acto knife to cut out the rectangle.

2. Position the church roof base in front of you with the 11- or 12-inch sides to your left and right. Along the 10-inch side closest to you, find the center (5 inches) and make a dot. Label this dot A. Along the 10-inch side farthest from you, find the center (5 inches) and make a dot. Label this dot B. Use a ruler to draw a straight line from dot A to dot B.

3. Lightly fold the roof base along this line to create a ridge. This folded base will rest on the two peaked walls of a basic peaked roof or on the one peaked wall of a scalloped facade roof. Label the peaked side of the roof "top." Later, you will apply texture to the "top" side of the roof.

COURTYARD BUILDING ROOFS

1. For the three courtyard building roof bases, measure and draw one piece in each of the following dimensions. If you plan to make the corrugated cardboard textured roof, draw the rectangle on the cardboard so that the lines of corrugation run in the same direction as the 2½-inch sides.

   ▶ 18 x 2½ inches
   ▶ 16 x 2½ inches
   ▶ 8 x 2½ inches

2. Position the 8-inch courtyard roof base in front of you with the 2½-inch sides to your left and right. From the lower left-hand corner, measure in 1¼ inches across the bottom and make a dot. Label this dot A. Draw a line from the top left-hand corner to dot A. Label this side of the roof "top." Later, you will apply texture to the "top" side of the roof. (Figure 27)

Walkways like this one at Santa Inés overlook the courtyard garden, where spices and herbs were grown.

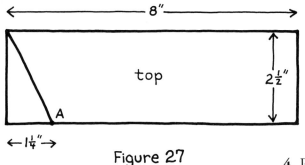

8"

top

2½"

A

1¼"

Figure 27

3. Position the 16-inch courtyard roof base in front of you with the 2½-inch sides to your left and right. From the lower left-hand corner, measure in 1¼ inches across the bottom and make a dot. Label this dot A. Draw a line from the top left-hand corner to dot A. Measure in 1¼ inches from the lower right-hand corner across the bottom and make a dot. Label this dot B. Draw a line from the top right corner to dot B. Label this side of the roof "top." Later, you will apply texture to the "top" side of the roof.

4. Position the 18-inch courtyard roof piece in front of you with the 2½-inch sides to your left and right. From the lower right-hand corner, measure in 1¼ inches across the bottom and make a dot. Label this dot A. Draw a line from the top right-hand corner to dot A. Label this side of the roof "top." Later, you will apply texture to the "top" side of the roof.

5. Use scissors or ask an adult to use an X-acto knife to cut out the roof bases for the courtyard buildings. On each of the three bases, trim along the diagonal lines that you have drawn. Discard the small triangular pieces that you have cut away.

6. If you decide you want an untextured roof, paint the cardboard with brownish red acrylic paint before attaching the roofs to the walls.

ADDING TEXTURE

Using pasta noodles or modeling clay you can add texture to your corrugated or noncorrugated roof base. To create a lasagna noodle textured roof, you need access to a stove to heat and soften the noodles. Another material that will give the roof a wavy, textured effect is red or brown modeling clay, which is available at most craft stores.

Corrugated Waves

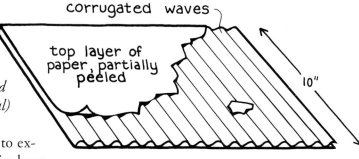

Figure 28

YOU WILL NEED:

corrugated cardboard roof bases • brownish red acrylic paint (optional) • paintbrush (optional)

1. Carefully peel off the thin top layer of paper to expose the corrugated waves. Removing the entire layer may be difficult—it is all right to leave some of the paper unpeeled. (Figure 28)
2. You may leave the roof the original tan color or paint it with brownish red acrylic paint.
3. Turn to Attaching the Church Roof on page 76 and 77 to learn how to attach the roofs to the walls.

Elbow Macaroni or Rigatoni

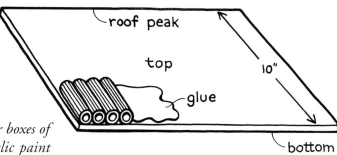

Figure 29

YOU WILL NEED:

corrugated or noncorrugated roof bases • 2 bags or boxes of elbow macaroni or rigatoni • brownish red acrylic paint • medium-size paintbrush • white household glue

1. Place the church roof base in front of you with the 10-inch sides to your left and right and the side labeled "top" facing up. Starting from the 12- or 11-inch side nearest you, apply a thin layer of glue to a 2-inch-square section of the roof base.
2. Position the macaroni or rigatoni side by side in rows to cover the glue, so that one end of the noodle faces the roof peak and the other faces the bottom of the roof. (Figure 29)

3. Apply glue to the next 2 inches of roof and repeat step 2. Go on applying glue and noodles until the roof base is covered.
4. Arrange the courtyard roofs in front of you horizontally, with the side labeled "top" up.
5. In the same way you attached macaroni or rigatoni to the church roof base, apply the noodles to each courtyard roof base.
6. Allow one or two hours for the glue to dry.
7. When the glue dries, paint the macaroni with brownish red acrylic paint.
8. Allow one to two hours for the paint to dry. Then learn how to attach the roofs to the walls by turning to the sections on pages 76 and 77.

Lasagna Noodles

YOU WILL NEED:

corrugated or noncorrugated roof bases • 2 boxes lasagna noodles • large kettle • kitchen tongs • paper towels • sharp kitchen knife • brownish red acrylic paint • medium paintbrush • scissors • white household glue

Preparing the Noodles

1. To make the noodles easier to work with, you will soften them a little. (You are not cooking them as much as you would if they were going to be eaten.) With an adult's help, fill a large kettle with water.
2. On the stove, heat water to a boil, add noodles, and then turn down the heat. Simmer the lasagna noodles for five minutes.
3. Have an adult remove the pan from the heat. The adult can use kitchen tongs to carefully lift noodles from the water and lay them on paper towels. After the lasagna noodles have cooled for

a few minutes, move all but three noodles to a cutting board. Have the adult use a sharp knife to slice the noodles in half lengthwise. (Do not slice the three still on paper towels.)

Attaching Noodles to the Roof Bases

1. Position the church roof base in front of you. Apply a thin layer of glue to cover one side of the roof base. Starting at the bottom of the roof, press a sliced noodle to the cardboard, aligning the noodle's wavy edge with the roof's bottom edge. If a noodle is not long enough to cover the roof's entire length, use part of another noodle to finish the row. (Figure 30)

2. Overlapping the previously glued noodle by ¼ inch, position another sliced noodle with wavy edge pointing towards the roof's bottom edge and glue it to the roof. Repeat this process, working your way up the roof to the peak.

3. Apply noodles to the other half of the roof, repeating steps 1 and 2.

4. When you have reached the roof's peak, glue one of the unsliced noodles lengthwise over the peak, making sure it is centered. If the roof is longer than the noodle, use part or all of another un-sliced noodle.

5. With scissors, trim any excess noodle from the sides of the roof so the noodles are flush with the edges of the cardboard.

6. Position one of the courtyard roof bases in front of you horizontally, with the side labeled "top" up (the wider edge should be farthest from you).

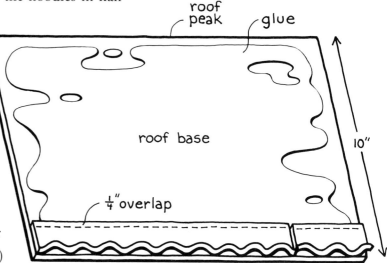

Figure 30

Adobe-clay tiles, first used at Mission San Luis Obispo, eventually covered the roofs of all 21 missions.

7. Apply a thin layer of glue to the roof base. Starting at the bottom of the roof, press a sliced noodle to the cardboard, aligning the noodle's wavy edge with the roof's bottom edge. If the noodle is not long enough to cover the roof's entire length, use part of another noodle to finish the row.

8. Overlapping the previous noodle by ¼ inch, glue one more sliced noodle to the courtyard roof with its wavy edge toward you and its sliced edge meeting or extending beyond the top of the roof base.

9. Trim any excess noodle from the top and sides of the courtyard roof base so noodles are flush with the edge of the cardboard. Do not trim the wavy edge.

10. Repeat steps 6 through 9 for the other courtyard roof bases. Allow one to two hours for the glue to dry.

11. When the glue dries, paint the lasagna noodles with brownish red acrylic paint. Allow one to two hours for the paint to dry, then learn how to attach the roofs to the walls by turning to pages 76 and 77.

Modeling Clay

YOU WILL NEED:
1 package red or brown modeling clay • waxed paper • rolling pin • corrugated or noncorrugated roof bases • dinner knife • cheese grater

1. On waxed paper, use a rolling pin to roll out one bar of clay into a quarter-inch-thick rectangle.

2. Lay the four cardboard roof bases on top of the clay, making sure there is at least ½ inch between all edges.

3. Using a dinner knife, cut the clay ¼ inch larger on all sides than the cardboard roof bases.

4. With the roof bases still on top of the cut-out clay, mold the quarter-inch clay excess so it covers the cardboard's edge.

5. Turn over the pieces and carefully peel off the waxed paper.

6. Press the large holes of a cheese grater into the clay so the round part of the Us in the pattern point towards the bottom of the roof. Lift off carefully. The raised waves left by the grater resemble adobe roof tiles.

7. Allow 24 to 48 hours for the clay to dry. Then learn how to attach the roofs to the walls in the next two sections.

ATTACHING THE CHURCH ROOF

1. To attach the church roof, apply pieces of tape vertically to the inside of the church walls. The tape must extend 1 inch above the walls. If you are attaching the roof to a church with a scalloped facade, only apply tape to the three unscalloped walls. (Figure 31)

2. Set one side of the church roof on top of your walls so that it overhangs the wall by ½ inch. Secure the roof by firmly pressing the tape extensions from step 1 to the roof's underside.

3. As you set down the other side of the roof, push the tape extensions toward the center of the church so the sticky side adheres to the underside of the roof.

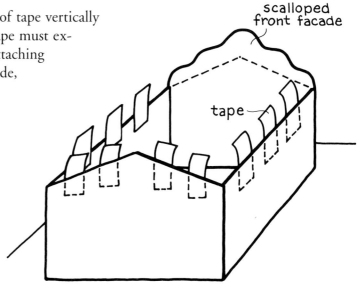

scalloped
front facade

tape

Figure 31

ATTACHING THE ROOFS OF THE COURTYARD BUILDINGS

1. To attach the courtyard buildings' roofs, every 3 inches, apply a piece of tape vertically to the inside of the mission walls. Make sure the pieces extend 1 inch above the walls.

2. Every 3 inches, apply a piece of tape vertically to the side of the courtyard walls nearest the mission walls. Make sure the pieces extend 1 inch above walls.

3. Attach the 16-inch roof piece first. Set the wider side down on the mission wall so that the roof just covers the entire top edge of the mission wall. The roof will overhang the courtyard wall by $\frac{1}{2}$ inch. Attach the tape extensions from the mission wall to the underside of the roof.

4. As you set down the narrower side of the roof, push the pieces of tape on the courtyard wall toward the mission wall so the sticky side of the tape adheres to the underside of the roof.

5. Follow steps 3 and 4 to attach the other two courtyard roofs. Align the angles to fit against the angles on the 16-inch piece.

DECORATING

When your mission buildings are complete, you may want to add finishing touches. You can bring your courtyard to life by choosing some or all of the options in Landscaping the Base and Adding Courtyard Features. Read through all of the options to see what you would like to include. Supply lists for each project come before each set of instructions.

LANDSCAPING THE BASE

There are many ways to landscape your base. You can color in dirt walkways, grass, trees, and shrubs on the cardboard or plywood base and on the sides of the mission walls or buildings. Or you can achieve a more realistic effect with some three-dimensional options. Apply glue to your walkways and cover with brown dirt, sand, small pebbles, or aquarium pebbles. Create grass, shrubbery, and small trees by gluing down dried moss or Easter-basket grass. When landscaping the base, do not cover any Xs you have made to mark the placement of courtyard items. You may add miniature hay bales, flour sacks, or figures of humans and farm animals to the courtyard. Wooden barrel-shaped beads may be used for water barrels. All of the following supplies are available at craft stores.

YOU WILL NEED:

- *wooden barrel-shaped bead (1 inch long)*
- *miniature hay bales*
- *miniature flour sacks*
- *figures of humans*
- *figures of farm animals*
- *miniature rabbits*
- *small birds*
- *dried moss*
- *sand or small pebbles*
- *small brown aquarium pebbles*
- *Easter-basket grass*
- *acrylic paint (brown, white, light blue, green)*
- *small paintbrush*
- *crayons or colored markers*
- *white household glue*

ADDING COURTYARD FEATURES

Nearly every mission courtyard included a dome-shaped oven, a large water fountain, wooden crosses, benches, bell posts, and water troughs for the animals. You may mold a dome-shaped oven from modeling dough, sand clay, or modeling clay, or you may create an oven by covering an egg carton cup with papier-mâché. Read through both sets of instructions and choose the method you like most. Decide which items you would like to include in your courtyard. Supply lists appear before each set of instructions.

Creating a Dome-Shaped Oven from Modeling Dough or Sand Clay

Feeding the several hundred people who lived at a mission took a long time and required a lot of space. Many of the women and girls at the mission spent most of the day preparing meals. Food was cooked or baked both indoors and outdoors. The outdoor ovens, called *hornitos,* were dome-shaped with a small opening on one side. You may make an oven from modeling dough, sand clay, or modeling clay. Turn to the recipes and instructions for making modeling dough (page 87) or sand clay (page 89). Covering an egg cup cut from an egg carton with papier-mâché also works well.

YOU WILL NEED:
modeling dough (dough left over from walls works fine), $\frac{1}{4}$ batch fresh sand clay, or brownish red modeling clay • waxed paper • ruler • dinner knife • acrylic paint (white and brown, or tan) • medium paintbrush

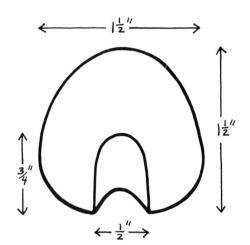

Figure 32

1. Between your palms, roll dough or clay into a 1$\frac{1}{2}$-inch ball.
2. Flatten the bottom of the ball by gently pressing it onto a small piece of waxed paper.
3. With your fingers, begin forming a mound that is 1$\frac{1}{2}$ inches in diameter and approximately 1$\frac{1}{2}$ inches high.
4. With a dinner knife, carve the outline for a small ($\frac{3}{4}$-inch-high by $\frac{1}{2}$-inch-wide), arched indentation, centered on the bottom front of the oven. Using the knife, scoop out the dough or clay in the indentation to create a tiny cave. (Figure 32)
5. Let the oven dry overnight. When the oven is completely dry, paint it tan. Allow one to two hours for the paint to dry before gluing the oven to the courtyard.
6. Apply a coat of glue to the bottom of the oven and gently press it onto the base to cover the X you drew earlier to mark its spot.

Creating a Papier-Mâché Oven

YOU WILL NEED:

1 egg-carton cup • 1 batch papier-mâché paste • strips of newspaper • scissors • acrylic paint (brown and white, or tan) • paintbrush • white household glue

1. Cut out one of the egg cups from an egg carton.
2. Using the paste and newspaper strips, papier-mâché the entire egg cup to increase the size of the dome.
3. Let the oven sit for two hours. Then cut an arched opening (³/₄ inch high by ¹/₂ inch wide), centered on the bottom front of the oven.
4. Let the papier-mâché dry overnight. When the oven is completely dry, paint it tan. Allow one to two hours for the paint to dry before gluing the oven to the courtyard.
5. Trim ¹/₄ inch from the bottom to create an even edge.
6. Apply a thin line of glue to the bottom edge of the oven, taking care not to get it on the painted walls. Gently press the oven onto the base to cover the X you drew earlier to mark its spot.

Creating a Water Fountain

Water fountains were popular features in courtyard gardens. Although most California mission water fountains were single-tiered, some were double-tiered. Some fountains stood alone, while others were centered on a tiled pool. Refer to the pictures in this book for ideas on making

An example of the double-tiered style, the fountain at San Buenaventura sits in a pool lined with mosaic tiles.

your fountain. Modeling dough, sand clay, or modeling clay are the easiest materials from which to construct a fountain.

YOU WILL NEED:
modeling dough (dough left over from walls works fine), ¹/₄ batch sand clay, or 1 bar modeling clay • waxed paper • ruler • white household glue • acrylic paint (brown, blue, and white, or tan and light blue) • small paintbrush

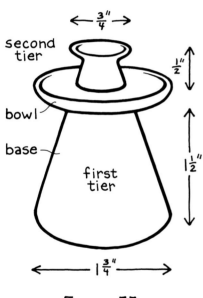

Figure 33

1. For a single-tiered fountain, roll the dough or clay between your palms into a 3-inch ball. If you plan to create a double-tiered fountain, you'll need another 1¹/₄-inch ball.
2. Place the 3-inch ball on a sheet of waxed paper.
3. With your fingers, begin forming a 1¹/₂-inch-high round base that starts out approximately 1³/₄ inches wide at the bottom and tapers to ³/₄ inch wide at the top.
4. On top of the base, work the dough or clay with your fingers to form a bowl 1³/₄ inches in diameter that resembles a bird bath. If you are building a single-tiered fountain, skip to step 8.
5. If you're constructing a double-tiered fountain, form the 1¹/₄-inch ball of dough or clay into a second base and bowl ³/₄ inch wide at the bottom and ¹/₂ inch tall.
6. Center the smaller base in the large bowl. (Figure 33)
7. With fingertips, carefully blend the dough or clay of the top base into the large bowl.
8. Let the fountain dry overnight. When the fountain is dry, paint the inside of the bowl(s) light blue and the rest of the fountain tan. If you plan to mix colors, turn to Paint on page 68.

9. If you have chosen to create a fountain centered in a shallow pool, on your cardboard or plywood base, paint the fountain pool light blue, leaving the center X unpainted. Allow one to two hours for the paint to dry.

10. Apply a coat of glue to the fountain's base. Center it over the X on your base and press down gently.

Creating Crosses

Large crosses were positioned around the courtyard grounds. Smaller crosses topped bell walls, bell towers, and church facades. Create large crosses using Popsicle sticks and small crosses with toothpicks.

YOU WILL NEED:
2 Popsicle sticks • 2 flat toothpicks • heavy scissors or garden shears • small scissors • pencil • ruler • fine sandpaper • waxed paper • white household glue • thumbtack or small nail

Large Crosses

1. Ask an adult to use heavy scissors or garden shears to cut off the rounded ends of two Popsicle sticks. On one stick, measure 3¼ inches from one end and make a mark with a pencil. On the other stick, measure 2¼ inches from one end and make a mark with a pencil. Have the adult cut the Popsicle sticks at the marks and throw away the remainder of the stick.

The chapel at San Francisco Solano has a basic peaked roof facade topped with a cross. A bell post takes the place of a bell tower or bell wall.

82

2. With sandpaper, lightly sand the ends of each piece.

3. Spread a piece of waxed paper across your work surface.

4. Three-quarters of an inch from one end of the longer piece, center and glue the shorter piece at a right angle to make a cross. Allow the glue to dry for 30 minutes.

5. Apply a line of glue to the bottom of the cross. Press the cross on the base and hold five minutes until the glue sets.

Small Crosses

1. Measure and make a mark on one of the toothpicks at $1\frac{1}{2}$ inches and another at 2 inches. Use scissors to cut toothpicks at the marks and throw away the remainder of the toothpick.

2. Three-quarters of an inch from one end of the longer piece, center and glue the shorter piece at a right angle to make a cross. Allow the glue to dry for 30 minutes.

3. To attach the cross, apply a thin coat of glue to the bottom $\frac{1}{2}$ inch of the cross.

4. The method you use for attaching the cross to the bell wall or church facade depends on the material from which you built the model.

   ▶ *For a bell tower dome or pyramid,* carefully pierce the top of the dome or pyramid with a thumbtack and insert the glued end of the cross $\frac{1}{4}$ inch into the hole. Hold the cross in place for five minutes until the glue sets and the cross stands straight on its own.

   ▶ *For a corrugated cardboard or foam corboard bell wall or church facade,* press the glued end of the cross about $\frac{1}{4}$ inch into the top of the facade or wall (make sure the cross is centered). Hold the cross in place for five minutes until the glue sets and the cross stands straight on its own.

Helpful Hint

If you will be inserting the cross into the top of a wet modeling dough or sand clay facade, turn back to Inserting a Cross on Top of the Bell Wall on page 47.

► *For a sugar cube church facade or bell wall,* press the glued end of the cross against the courtyard side of the top cube. Hold the cross in place for five minutes until the glue sets and the cross stands straight on its own. If you did not insert a cross into the modeling dough or sand clay church facade or bell wall when the walls were still wet, you may glue a cross to the courtyard side of the facade or bell wall using this method.

You can add details to your court-yard by making benches out of Popsicle sticks. The benches at Santa Inés were constructed of strong wood.

Building a Bench

YOU WILL NEED:
1 Popsicle stick • heavy scissors or garden shears • ruler • pencil • fine sandpaper • waxed paper • white house-hold glue • acrylic paint (brown) • small paintbrush

1. Ask an adult to use heavy scissors or garden shears to cut off the rounded ends of the Popsicle stick. Measure and mark with a pencil at $1^1/_4$ inches, at $1^3/_4$ inches, and at $2^1/_4$ inches.
2. Have the adult cut the stick at the marks you have made. You will have one $1^1/_4$-inch piece and two $^1/_2$-inch pieces.
3. With sandpaper, lightly sand the ends of each piece.
4. Spread a piece of waxed paper on your work surface, and on the paper lay flat the $1^1/_4$-inch piece lengthwise in front of you.
5. Apply a thin line of glue to one sanded edge of each $^1/_2$-inch piece.
6. Glue one of the short pieces about $^1/_8$ inch in from the left-hand end of the long piece, forming a right angle. (Figure 34)

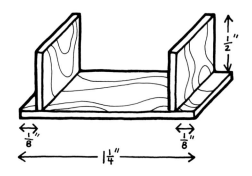

Figure 34

7. Glue the other short piece approximately $\frac{1}{8}$ inch in from the right-hand end of the long piece, forming a right angle.

8. Allow the bench to dry for one hour. You may want to paint the bench brown before gluing it to the courtyard. Allow one to two hours for the paint to dry. Then apply a thin line of glue to the bottom of the bench legs, turn the bench right-side up, and position it in the courtyard. Gently press the bench to the base and hold for five minutes until the glue sets.

Making a Water Trough

YOU WILL NEED:
2 Popsicle sticks • heavy scissors or garden shears • ruler • pencil • fine sandpaper • waxed paper • white household glue • acrylic paint (brown, blue, and white or light blue) • small paintbrush

1. Ask an adult to use heavy scissors or garden shears to cut off the rounded ends of the Popsicle sticks. Measure and use a pencil to mark off five pieces—three $1\frac{1}{2}$-inch pieces and two pieces that are a little wider than the Popsicle stick.

2. Have the adult cut the sticks at the marks you have made.

3. With sandpaper, lightly sand the ends of each piece.

4. Spread a piece of waxed paper on your work surface, and on the paper, lay flat one of the $1\frac{1}{2}$-inch pieces. Along the stick's long dimension, apply glue to both thin edges.

5. To create the long sides of the trough, align one $1\frac{1}{2}$-inch piece alongside each of the thin glued edges. Press pieces to the glue and hold for five minutes until the glue has set. (Figure 35)

6. Let glue dry for 30 minutes.

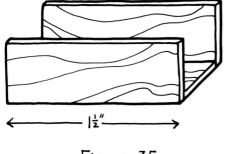

←—— $1\frac{1}{2}''$ ——→

Figure 35

7. Apply glue along the three edges on the right- and left-hand ends of the trough.
8. Position one of the short pieces at each end to close off the trough. Make sure the end pieces are even with the top of the trough. Press each piece to the glue and hold for five minutes until the glue has set. (Figure 36)
9. Allow glue to dry for one hour. You may want to paint the outside of the trough brown and the inside blue to look like water. Paint the trough before you attach it to the base. Allow one to two hours for the paint to dry. Then apply a thin line of glue to the bottom of the trough, turn the trough right-side up, and position it in the courtyard. Gently press the trough to the base and hold for five minutes until the glue sets.

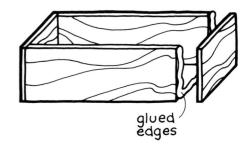

glued edges

Figure 36

Creating a Bell Post

Mission bells not only hung from bell walls or bell towers, but also from doorway-shaped bell posts in the courtyard.

YOU WILL NEED:
2 brown pipe cleaners • ruler • 1 purchased bell (³/₄ inch) or 1 cardboard bell, prepared for hanging • white household glue

1. To create a bell post, bend each of the pipe cleaners 2 inches from one end to create a right angle.
2. Lay the two pipe cleaners on the work surface in front of you so the bent ends are farthest from you and point toward each other, creating the shape of a doorway. If you are using a purchased bell, thread the short side of one pipe cleaner through the top of the bell.

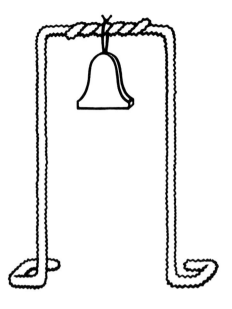

Figure 37

3. To connect the pipe cleaners, twist together the ends of the short sides. If you are hanging cardboard bells, loop the string around the center of the doorway and tie a double knot. Trim the ends of the string closely to the knot. (Figure 37)

4. One inch from the bottom of each side of the doorway, bend the pipe cleaner three times to create a tiny square base for attaching the bell post to the base. Apply glue to the two square bases, position the bell post in the courtyard, and press it to the base. Hold the bell post for five minutes until the glue sets.

RECIPES

If you choose to build your model using modeling dough or sand clay, you will need to make the dough or clay. Both recipes require you to use a stove, so you will need an adult's assistance. Be sure to cut out the pattern pieces for all of the walls before making the dough or clay. Fresh dough or clay is more pliable and easier to work with.

MODELING DOUGH

If you want your mission to look like adobe bricks, add red food coloring when you mix the dough. If you leave out the food coloring, the finished modeling dough mission will appear to be coated with limestone. Three batches of modeling dough should be enough to make your model's mission walls, church walls, courtyard walls, and all other elements made from dough. To keep the dough from drying out, mix one batch at a time, using all of it before mixing the next one. If necessary, you may store dough in a tightly sealed plastic bag in the refrigerator until you are ready to use it. Keep any dough you have left after making the walls. You will be able to use the dough later to create features to decorate the courtyard. Ask an adult to help you make the dough.

YOU WILL NEED:
small saucepan • large glass or plastic mixing bowl • large wooden or metal spoon • measuring cups (¹/₄ cup, ¹/₂ cup) • measuring spoons (1 teaspoon, ¹/₂ teaspoon)

Ingredients:
³/₄ cup flour (not self-rising) • ¹/₂ cup salt • 1¹/₂ teaspoons powdered alum • 1¹/₂ teaspoons vegetable oil • ¹/₂ cup boiling water • red food coloring (optional)

Making the Dough

1. With adult supervision, pour the water into the saucepan and bring it to a boil over high heat.
2. As the water heats, combine flour, salt, and alum in the mixing bowl.
3. Carefully add vegetable oil and boiling water to the dry ingredients in the mixing bowl. If you have decided that you want your mission to be the color of adobe bricks, add a few drops of red food coloring.
4. Stir rapidly with a spoon until everything is well blended. Your modeling dough is ready to use when it doesn't stick to the sides of the bowl and is cool enough to handle.
5. Return to Modeling Dough or Sand Clay Mission on page 23 or Modeling Dough or Sand Clay Bell Wall (page 46) or Bell Tower (page 59) to learn how to create wall pieces from the dough.

SAND CLAY

Three of the California missions were built of sandstone—San Juan Capistrano, Santa Bárbara, and San Carlos Borromeo de Carmelo. The sand in the clay gives this model a rough, cracked texture, resembling the coarseness of sandstone. Four batches should be enough to make your model's mission walls, church walls, courtyard walls, and all other clay elements. To keep the sand clay from drying out, mix one batch at a time, using all of it before mixing the next one. Sand clay cannot be stored, so make sure you have time to use an entire batch at one sitting. Ask an adult to help you make the clay.

The limestone stucco has eroded from these walls at Mission San Miguel Arcángel, exposing the adobe bricks.

YOU WILL NEED:

large saucepan without a nonstick coating • large glass or ceramic mixing bowl • large wooden spoon • measuring cup (1 cup)

Ingredients:

2 cups coarse sand • 1 cup cornstarch • 1 cup water

Making the Clay

1. Before you put the saucepan on the stove, mix sand, cornstarch, and water in the pan until all the cornstarch dissolves.
2. With adult supervision, put saucepan on the stove over medium heat. Stirring constantly, cook until the clay begins to clump together and all the water is absorbed. (This will take about five minutes.)
3. Turn the warm clay into the mixing bowl. Clay is ready to use when it is cool enough to handle.
4. Go to Modeling Dough or Sand Clay Mission on page 23 or Modeling Dough or Sand Clay Bell Wall (page 46) or Bell Tower (page 59) to learn how to create wall pieces from the clay.

PART TWO—LAYOUTS

NEW SPAIN BECAME THE COUNTRY OF MEXICO IN 1821.
The Mexican government thought the Roman Catholic Church had
too much power in Alta California. The Franciscans controlled valu-
able farmland that the Mexican government wanted its citizens to have.

In the 1830s, laws passed by the Mexican government took away
mission lands and put them under the authority of civil administrators. The government assigned these officials the responsibility of dis-
tributing mission properties fairly among Indians, settlers of Spanish
descent, and non-Spanish settlers. But some administrators were dis-
honest. They often sold lands promised to Indians to Spanish settlers
for a fraction of their actual worth.

When padres and Indian laborers left the missions, many of the
buildings fell into decay. Over time, people took mission furnishings,
such as bells, roof tiles, fountains, and statues. In the 1880s, artists
sketched and painted mission ruins, and authors wrote books and ar-
ticles that glorified the mission era of California's history. This public-
ity sparked a renewed interest in the missions.

From the 1890s to the present, many of the missions have been rebuilt. Because of the extensive rebuilding and renovation, the missions
don't always resemble their original design. In addition, much of the
farmland that had once supported the people on the missions has long
since been sold. Despite these drawbacks, each year thousands of people visit California's missions to explore an important and controver-
sial period in California's history.

The mission chain stretched along El Camino Reál (the King's Road), following the coast of California from San Diego northward to Sonoma.

Highlights of Present-Day California

- City
- Mission (see list below left)
- County
- El Camino Reál
- U.S. highway

Miles
0 20 40 60 80 100

Kilometers
0 40 80 120

CALIFORNIA MISSIONS

A San Francisco Solano
B San Rafael Arcángel
C San Francisco de Asís
D San José
E Santa Clara de Asís
F Santa Cruz
G San Juan Bautista
H San Carlos Borromeo
I Soledad
J San Antonio de Padua
K San Miguel Arcángel
L San Luis Obispo
M La Purísima
N Santa Inés
O Santa Bárbara
P San Buenaventura
Q San Fernando Rey
R San Gabriel Arcángel
S San Juan Capistrano
T San Luis Rey de Francia
U San Diego de Alcalá

NEVADA

Sacramento

SIERRA NEVADA

CALIFORNIA

San Joaquin Valley

MOJAVE DESERT

PACIFIC OCEAN

Bodega Bay
Sonoma
San Pablo Bay
San Rafael
SAN FRANCISCO PRESIDIO
Alcatraz I.
San Francisco
Fremont
San Francisco Bay
San Jose
Santa Clara
Guadalupe R.
San Lorenzo R.
Pajaro R.
Santa Cruz
Monterey Bay
San Juan Bautista
MONTEREY PRESIDIO
Monterey
Carmel
Carmel R.
Salinas R.
Soledad
King City
San Antonio R.
Nacimiento R.
San Miguel

San Luis Obispo
La Purisima
Lompoc
Solvang
Santa Ynez
Santa Ynez R.
Point Conception
Santa Barbara
SANTA BARBARA CHANNEL
Ventura R.
Ventura
VENTURA COUNTY
SANTA BARBARA PRESIDIO
Santa Clara R.
San Fernando
San Gabriel R.
San Gabriel
Los Angeles R.
Santa Monica Bay
Santa Ana R.
Los Angeles
ORANGE COUNTY
San Juan Capistrano
Oceanside
San Diego R.
San Diego
SAN DIEGO PRESIDIO
San Diego Bay

SANTA BARBARA ISLANDS
San Miguel I.
Santa Rosa I.
Santa Cruz I.
Anacapa Is.
Santa Barbara I.
Santa Catalina I.
San Nicolas I.
San Clemente I.

UNITED STATES
MEXICO

MEXICO
BAJA CALIFORNIA

PACIFIC OCEAN

Sacramento River
Stanislaus R.
San Joaquin River

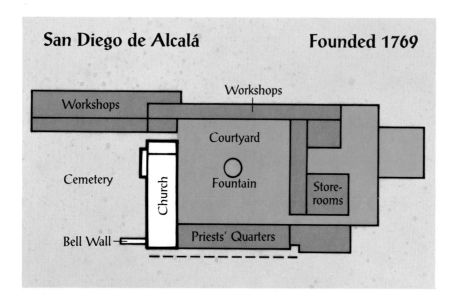

San Diego de Alcalá

Founded 1769

Workshops

Workshops

Courtyard

Cemetery

Church

Fountain

Store-rooms

Bell Wall

Priests' Quarters

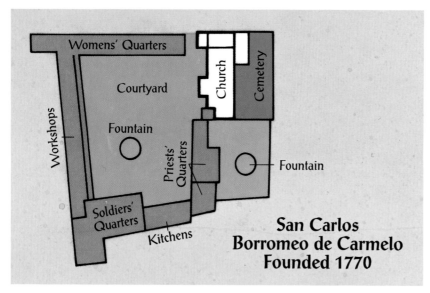

Womens' Quarters

Courtyard

Church

Cemetery

Workshops

Fountain

Priests' Quarters

Fountain

Soldiers' Quarters

Kitchens

**San Carlos
Borromeo de Carmelo
Founded 1770**

Father Serra, head of the mission system, founded San Diego de Alcalá in 1769. The mission is still an active church in the port city of San Diego.

The French explorer Jean François de Galaup was the first to lead non-Spanish ships to a Spanish mission when he visited San Carlos Borromeo de Carmelo in 1786. Established in 1770, the mission attracts visitors to the small city of Carmel.

The facade, or front *(above)*, of Mission San Gabriel has withstood strong earthquakes since its founding in 1771. During its peak years, the mission produced wine, soap, candles, and hides.

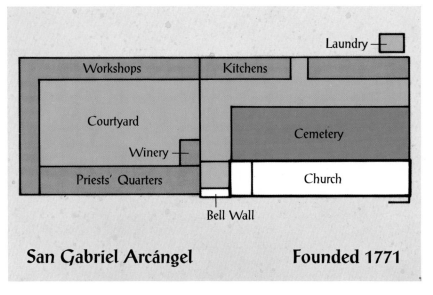

Laundry

Workshops

Kitchens

Courtyard

Cemetery

Winery

Priests' Quarters

Church

Bell Wall

San Gabriel Arcángel   **Founded 1771**

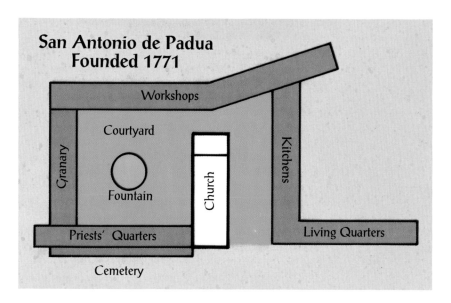

San Antonio de Padua
Founded 1771

Workshops

Courtyard

Granary

Fountain

Church

Kitchens

Priests' Quarters

Living Quarters

Cemetery

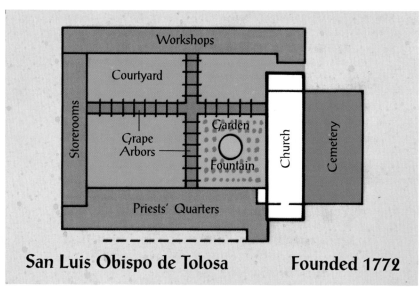

Workshops

Courtyard

Storerooms

Grape Arbors

Garden

Fountain

Church

Cemetery

Priests' Quarters

San Luis Obispo de Tolosa   Founded 1772

Mission San Antonio de Padua, set up in 1771 near the San Antonio River, was rebuilt a short distance from San Miguel Creek after the river dried up.

For the site of San Luis Obispo de Tolosa, Father Serra chose an area inhabited by the Chumash. The fifth California mission, San Luis Obispo was founded in 1772.

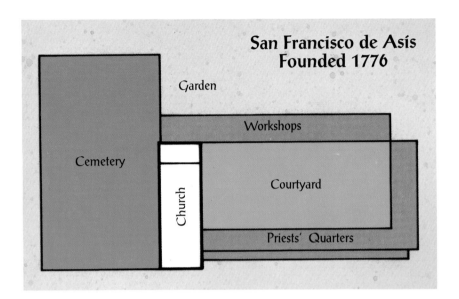

San Francisco de Asís
Founded 1776

Garden

Cemetery

Church

Workshops

Courtyard

Priests' Quarters

Set up in 1776, San Francisco de Asís is still used for baptisms and other special religious services in the city of San Francisco. Beside the original adobe mission chapel (left) is the larger and more ornate Mission Dolores Basilica.

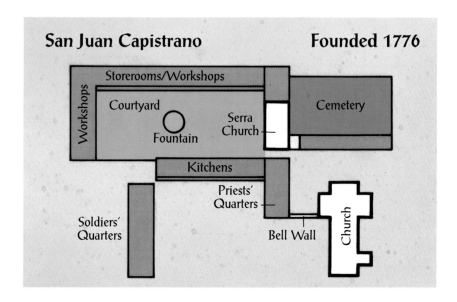

San Juan Capistrano   Founded 1776

Storerooms/Workshops

Workshops

Courtyard

Fountain

Serra
Church

Cemetery

Kitchens

Priests'
Quarters

Soldiers'
Quarters

Bell Wall

Church

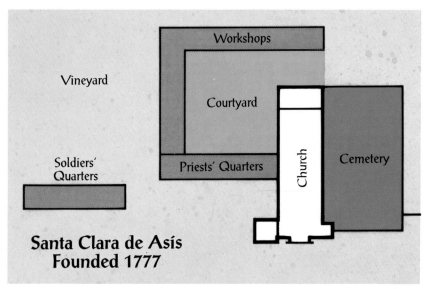

Vineyard

Workshops

Courtyard

Soldiers'
Quarters

Priests' Quarters

Church

Cemetery

Santa Clara de Asís
Founded 1777

Springtime visitors to San Juan Capistrano, a southern California mission founded in 1776, may witness the annual arrival of cliff swallows. The birds usually show up around March 19.

Between 1851 and 1912, Santa Clara de Asís, established in 1777, was used as a private college where teachers held classes in the remains of mission buildings. The church is still the center of the University of Santa Clara.

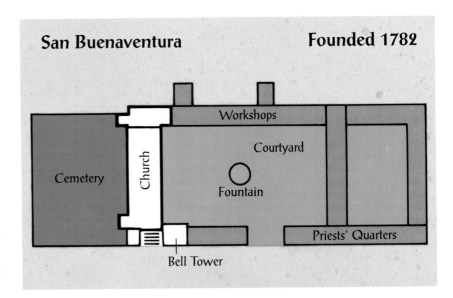

San Buenaventura   Founded 1782

Workshops

Courtyard

Cemetery

Church

Fountain

Priests' Quarters

Bell Tower

The site for San Buenaventura, a southern mission set up in 1782, was chosen because it was close to coastal Chumash villages.

Missionaries at Santa Bárbara, founded in 1786, used glass beads, tools, and blankets to encourage the Chumash to build the mission and to be baptized.

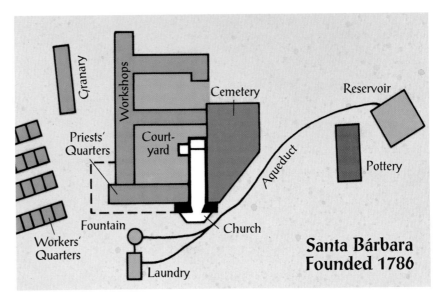

Granary

Workshops

Cemetery

Reservoir

Priests' Quarters

Court- yard

Aqueduct

Pottery

Fountain

Workers' Quarters

Laundry

Church

Santa Bárbara
Founded 1786

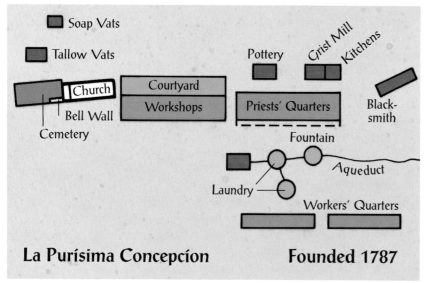

Soap Vats

Tallow Vats

Church

Bell Wall

Cemetery

Courtyard

Workshops

Pottery

Grist Mill

Kitchens

Priests' Quarters

Blacksmith

Fountain

Aqueduct

Laundry

Workers' Quarters

La Purísima Concepcíon   **Founded 1787**

(Above) *The facade of Mission Santa Bárbara was built in the neoclassical style that was popular in Europe in the late 1700s.* (Left) *La Purísima Concepción, founded in 1787, was rebuilt at a different spot in 1813 after earthquakes and floods destroyed the original site.*

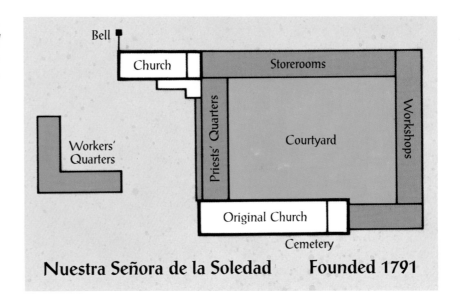

**Santa Cruz
Founded 1791**

Workshops

Granary

Courtyard

Orchard

Cemetery

Church

Priests' Quarters

Living
Quarters

Soon after building Mission Santa Cruz in 1791, the Franciscans moved the settlement uphill to escape flooding from the San Lorenzo River.

A troubled mission from its founding, Nuestra Señora de la Soledad was built in 1791 in a valley that an early expedition mistook for Monterey Bay.

Bell

Church

Storerooms

Priests' Quarters

Courtyard

Workshops

Workers' Quarters

Original Church

Cemetery

Nuestra Señora de la Soledad   Founded 1791

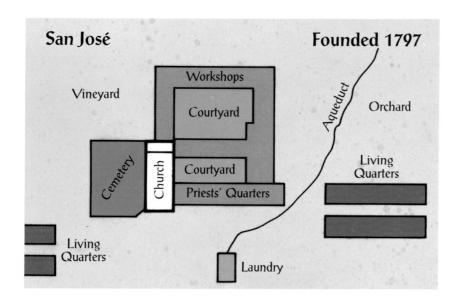

San José, set up in 1797, was the home of an Indian laborer named Estanislao, who led a revolt against the mission in 1828.

San Juan Bautista, founded in 1797, was named for Saint John the Baptist.

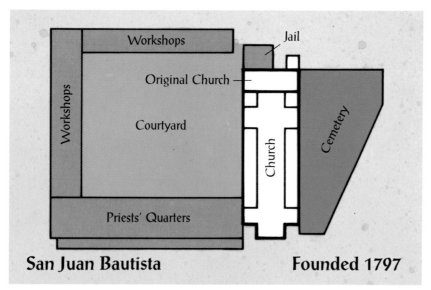

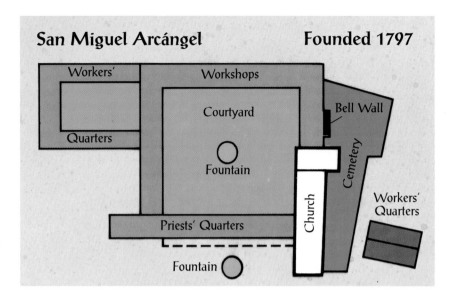

San Miguel Arcángel **Founded 1797**

Workers'

Workshops

Courtyard

Bell Wall

Quarters

Cemetery

Fountain

Church

Workers' Quarters

Priests' Quarters

Fountain

Situated near the joining of the Salinas and Nacimiento Rivers, Mission San Miguel Arcángel was successful from its founding in 1797.

Established in 1797, San Fernando Rey de España had facilities for overnight guests and was a favorite stopping place for weary travelers.

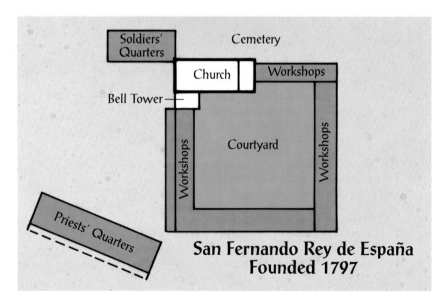

Soldiers' Quarters

Cemetery

Church

Workshops

Bell Tower

Workshops

Courtyard

Workshops

Priests' Quarters

San Fernando Rey de España
Founded 1797

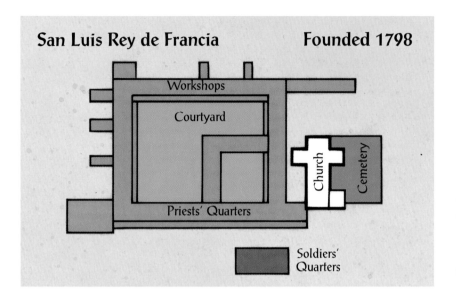

San Luis Rey de Francia   **Founded 1798**

Workshops

Courtyard

Church

Cemetery

Priests' Quarters

Soldiers' Quarters

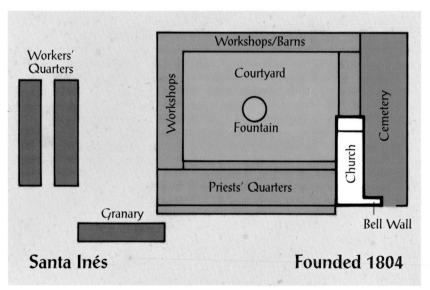

Workers' Quarters

Workshops/Barns

Courtyard

Workshops

Fountain

Cemetery

Church

Priests' Quarters

Granary

Bell Wall

Santa Inés   **Founded 1804**

Father Antonio Peyri ran Mission San Luis Rey de Francia for more than 30 years. Established in 1798, the settlement produced food and goods to supply the mission and to trade.

One year after its founding in 1804, Mission Santa Inés didn't have enough Indian workers to succeed. Most of the Native Americans in the area had remained in their villages.

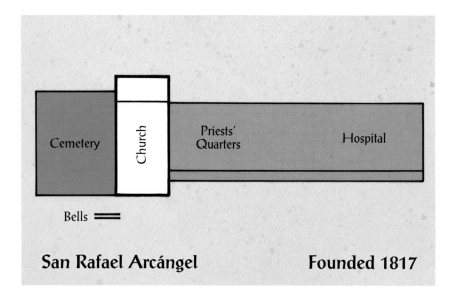

San Rafael Arcángel **Founded 1817**

San Rafael Arcángel was built in 1817 as a hospital for Mission San Francisco de Asís.

Constructed in 1823, San Francisco Solano was the last of the missions to be founded. In ruins by the 1880s, the mission was bought by the California Historical Landmarks League, which began to rebuild it in 1903.

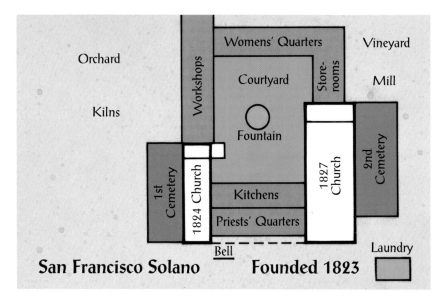

San Francisco Solano **Founded 1823**

INDEX

bases, 6–12; bell tower wall, 10–11; church wall, 9; courtyard wall, 9–10; finishing touches, 12; mission walls, 7–8. *See also* placement lines

bells, 39–42; hanging, 40–42, 45, 46–47, 58

bell tower: arches, 52–53; attaching roof to, 55; attaching to base, 54–55, 58–59, 62; constructing, 51–55, 59–60, 60–63; pattern pieces for, 51–53, 60; placement lines for, 10–11; second tier, 55. *See also* dome top; milk carton bell tower; pyramid top

bell wall: arches, 44–45; attaching to base, 45–46, 48, 50–51; constructing, 43–46, 46–47, 48–50; pattern pieces for, 43–45, 48–49

cardboard mission: assembling, 19–20; attaching to base, 21–23; exterior treatments, 65–66; finishing, 23; walls, 13–23

church walls: cardboard or foam corboard, 16–18, 20, 22; modeling dough or sand clay, 24; placement lines for, 9; sugar cube, 28–29, 30–34, 35, 37–38

courtyard walls: arches, 14–16, 28, 39; cardboard or foam corboard, 14, 20, 21; modeling dough or sand clay, 24; placement lines for, 9–10; sugar cube, 28, 35

decorating, 78–87

dome top, 63–64

end wall: cardboard or foam corboard, 19, 22–23; modeling dough or sand clay, 24; sugar cube, 36–37

exterior treatments, 65–68

finishing touches, 12, 23, 26, 39, 78–87

foam corboard mission: assembling, 19–20; attaching to base, 21–23; exterior treatments, 65–66; finishing, 23; walls, 13–19

La Purísima Concepción, 26, 98

milk carton bell tower, 56–58

mission walls: cardboard or foam corboard, 14, 19, 21; modeling dough or sand clay, 24; placement lines for, 7–8; sugar cube, 28, 36, 37–39

modeling dough: attaching bells to, 46–47; pattern pieces for, 24; recipe for, 87–88; walls, 23–26, 66

Nuestra Señora de la Soledad, 99

paint, 23, 26, 68

papier-mâché: 23, 63–64, 66–68, 80

paper pattern pieces for: bell tower, 51–52, 60; bell walls, 43–45, 48–49; modeling dough or sand clay walls, 24; sugar cube walls, 27–28

peaked roof: 16–17, 28, 37–38

placement lines, 7–12

pyramid top, 64–65

roofs: 69–77. *See also* peaked roof; scalloped facade

San Antonio de Padua, 16, 94

San Buenaventura, 10, 80, 97

San Carlos Borromeo de Carmelo, 16, 33, 62, 65, 89, 92

sand clay: attaching bells to, 46–47; pattern pieces for, 24; recipe for, 89; walls, 23–26

San Diego de Alcalá, 4, 16, 24, 92

San Fernando Rey de España, 101

San Francisco de Asís, 95

San Francisco Solano, 82, 103

San Gabriel Arcángel, 93

San José, 100

San Juan Bautista, 48, 100

San Juan Capistrano, 5, 12, 43, 65, 89, 96

San Luis Obispo de Tolosa, 75, 94

San Luis Rey de Francia, 16, 50, 102

San Miguel Arcángel, 14, 67, 88–89, 101

San Rafael Arcángel, 34, 103

Santa Bárbara, 63, 65, 89, 97, 98

Santa Clara de Asís, 25, 96

Santa Cruz, 99

Santa Inés, 39, 70, 84, 102

scalloped facade, 16, 17–18, 28, 38

sugar cube mission: assembling, 29–33; attaching to base, 34–37; exterior treatment for, 66; finishing, 39; pattern pieces for, 27–29; walls, 29–39

texture, 25, 71–77